JAPANESE STORIES

FOR LANGUAGE LEARNERS

ショートストーリーで学ぶ日本語

Bilingual Stories in Japanese and English

Anne McNulty & Eriko Sato

Illustrated by Rose Goldberg

TUTTLE Publishing

Tokyo | Rutland, Vermont | Singapore

Contents

Introduction

Stories are powerful. They let us travel across time and space in a flash, feel emotions of people we have never met, and discover truth in an infinite number of dimensions. *Japanese Stories for Language Learners* takes you through a cultural and linguistic journey through five Japanese short stories. The first two stories are from traditional Japanese folktales: "*Urashima Tarō*" ("Urashima Taro") and "*Yuki Onna*" ("Snow Woman"). The following three stories are from modern Japanese literature: "*Kumo no Ito*" ("The Spider's Thread") by Ryūnosuke Akutagawa (1892–1927), "*Oborekaketa Kyōdai*" ("The Siblings Who Almost Drowned") by Takeo Arishima (1878–1923) and "*Serohiki no Gōshu*" ("Gauche the Cellist") by Kenji Miyazawa (1896–1933).

Japanese Stories for Language Learners can be used by learners of Japanese at intermediate and advanced levels: They can learn vocabulary and grammar while reading these stories using the glossaries, grammar notes, and exercises provided for each story. This book can also be used by non-language learners: English speakers can read the English translation while Japanese speakers can read Japanese original text to appreciate Japanese literature and deepen their understanding of Japanese culture. We can learn interesting facts from history books and newspapers, but it is difficult to feel the raw emotions of people who lived at a different time or in a different place. Reading literature and learning a new language opens doors to a new world.

Japanese Stories for Language Learners was created by a teacher-student team in Japanese and translation studies courses at Stony Brook University. This collaboration made way for a unique blend of the teacher's perspective and the student's perspective to prepare vocabulary and grammar notes, exercises and discussion questions. Following the theories of translation studies, it also combined native Japanese and English intuition to best represent the pragmatic nuances of both languages. As an outcome of the teacher-student collaboration, this book can assist those who are interested in communicating across different cultures. The team sincerely hopes that all readers of this book will be able to extract some of the spirit of Japan from each story, broaden their horizons, and further enrich their lives.

Structure of the Book

Japanese Stories for Language Learners has the following components:

Japanese Texts

The book provides five stories in total. The first two stories are simplified versions of traditional folktales, *"Urashima Tarō"* and *"Yuki Onna."* They are useful warm-ups to authentic Japanese literature. The following three stories are Japanese literature from the early 20th century: *"Kumo no Ito," "Oborekaketa Kyōdai"* and *"Serohiki no Gōshu."* They are unabridged and unedited, apart from the addition of furigana. They are challenging, but learners of Japanese will be able to feel a sense of achievement after reading them: They can claim to have read original Japanese literature written by notable Japanese authors.

Translation

English translations are placed right next to their corresponding Japanese text appearing on facing pages so that the readers can compare them easily. Accordingly, the English translations provided in this book are faithful to the Japanese texts, but were also made as natural as possible. Learners of Japanese are recommended not to read the translation first. They should read the Japanese text and think about the meaning, before looking at the English translation.

Translator's Notes

Many Japanese words and phrases cannot be easily translated into English because Japanese is linguistically and culturally distinct from English. Certain elements such as onomatopoeia, terms of address, proper names, pronouns, culture-specific terms, and puns cause problems for translators. Furthermore, differences in rhetorical style and sentence structure also cause a problem in conveying hidden pragmatic information. This section shows the strategies that were taken for solving or minimizing such translation problems in this book. They reveal insights into language, language use and culture in Japan and in English-speaking societies.

Vocabulary and Expressions

This section provides the meanings, usage, and grammar notes for words and expressions that appear in the story. Each item is specified in kana, kanji with furigana and also in romanized form. Accordingly, this section helps not only language learners who want to expand their vocabulary and grammar knowledge, but also non-language learners who do not speak Japanese. For example, non-language learners can pick up a few key words for each story by looking at the romanized form of the words. This way they can directly experience the language used in a literary context.

Brief grammar explanations appear after [GRAMMAR] and are followed by an example sentence. The descriptions of mimetic words appear after [MIMETIC] (a variety of sound symbolism including onomatopoeia). Uncommonly used kanji that appear in the last three stories are provided with alternative commonly used kanji, if any, after [=] .

Exercises

This section gives multiple-choice questions about vocabulary and grammar in order to strengthen Japanese-language skills. They are arranged in such a way that the readers can quickly recall the storyline as they work on each question in order. The questions in this section are represented only in Japanese.

Discussion Questions

This section provides a few open-ended and thought-provoking questions, to help readers deepen their understanding and appreciation of the story, freely explore hidden themes, relate them to their own lives, and talk about them with their family, friends or classmates. Discussion questions are presented only in English. The readers can discuss these questions in English or Japanese. The point is to explore and share ideas openly without being limited by Japanese language skills.

Answer Key

An Answer Key provides the correct options for the multiple-choice questions in the Exercises.

Audio CD

The accompanying audio CD provides the oral narrative of the Japanese stories recorded by a native speaker of Japanese. Learners of Japanese can listen to one paragraph at a time and practice reading it aloud. They can also record their own pronunciation, and compare it with the recording by the native speaker. Through this kind of practice, learners can develop authentic pronunciation, intonation and rhythm in Japanese.

Non-language learners can also listen to the CD to feel the emotion that comes from the sounds as they imagine the context of the story.

About the Stories

"*Urashima Tarō*" ("Urashima Taro") is a Japanese folktale about a fisherman whose family name was *Urashima* and whose given name was *Tarō*. It is based on a legend recorded in multiple pieces of literature dating to the 8th century such as the *Nihonshoki* (*The Chronicles of Japan*) and *Man'yōshū* (*Collection of Ten Thousand Leaves*). Urashima Taro rescues a turtle that was being bullied by a group of children. In return, that turtle comes back to him a few years later and guides him to the Palace of the Dragon King at the bottom of the sea. Urashima Taro enjoys staying there so much that he forgets about time. The story promotes cherishing and protecting the lives of all creatures, and also presents a myth about time: when one is having a great time, he forgets about time. One's familiar village becomes a strange place after many years. Neighbors and familiar landmarks in the village may become impossible to find. The world changes very quickly, and we may occasionally feel that we are like Urashima Taro when we revisit our home country.

"*Yuki-onna*" ("Snow Woman") is a Japanese folktale about a beautiful woman that appears on snowy nights and freezes people to death, but did not kill a young man named Minokichi. The legend appears to have existed in the Muromachi period (1336–1573). Japan is famous for producing psychological thrillers and horror stories. This story is one of them. It makes us wonder why she kills people, why she did not kill Minokichi, and what she actually wants.

"*Kumo no Ito*" ("The Spider's Thread") was written by Ryūnosuke Akutagawa (1892–1927). Akutagawa graduated from Tokyo Imperial University (currently University of Tokyo), where he studied English literature. He is regarded as the "father of the Japanese short story." "*Kumo no Ito*" is about the afterlife of a villain named Kandata. Do you think cold-blooded criminals and murderers may have a hidden compassion for others? If so, should they be salvaged? That is what Buddha wondered one day. The story is short and simple, but gives us an unforgettable impression on human nature, demonstrated by the events in the Pond of Blood in Hell where the spider's thread was dropped down from above. After reading this story, you might think twice before killing that bug on the floor.

"Oborekaketa Kyōdai" ("The Siblings Who Almost Drowned") was written by Takeo Arishima (1878–1923). Arishima was the son of a high-ranking government official in Japan. He studied at Sapporo Agricultural College, Haverford College, and Harvard University, converted to Christianity, and gradually adopted socialism. *"Oborekaketa Kyōdai"* is probably based on Arishima's real-life experiences. The description of waves in this story is very vivid and frightening; the reader becomes immersed in the oceanic scene. In the middle of the ocean amidst gargantuan waves, would you swim towards shore to seek help, or away from shore towards your drowning little sister? This story makes us think about human nature and how guilt can shadow our lives.

"Serohiki no Gōshu" ("Gauche the Cellist") was written by Kenji Miyazawa (1896–1933). Miyazawa was born into a wealthy family engaged in the pawnbroking business in northern Japan. He was a poet and an author of children's literature, but was also a devoted scientist (agronomy, biology, geology, and astronomy), artist (painter, cellist, and composer, lover of opera and classical music), foreign language learner (English, German and Esperanto), devout Buddhist, and a social activist. He worked hard to improve the living conditions of poor farmers in northern Japan. Most of his poems and stories were discovered and published posthumously. This story is about a musician named Gōshu. It is not known where his name, Gōshu, originates; it does not sound like a Japanese name or any common European name. The story begins with the scene where Gōshu is scolded by the conductor during a rehearsal. The artistry of music strongly manifests itself and moves an audience's emotions, but only after intensive practice. The relationship between Gōshu and the animals that visit him several nights before the performance gradually changes him and becomes precious to him.

References

Stories

Urashima Tarō: http://www.aozora.gr.jp/cards/000329/files/3390_33153.html (downloaded on September 16, 2017)

Yuki Onna: http://www.aozora.gr.jp/cards/000154/files/4947_16626.html (downloaded on September 16, 2017)

Kumo no Ito: http://www.aozora.gr.jp/cards/000879/files/92_14545.html (downloaded on September 16, 2017)

Oborekaketa Kyōdai: http://www.aozora.gr.jp/cards/000025/files/215_20451.html (downloaded on September 16, 2017)

Serohiki no Gōshu: http://www.aozora.gr.jp/cards/000081/files/470_15407.html (downloaded on September 16, 2017)

Translation

Nida, E. A. (1964) *Toward a science of translating*. Leiden: E. J. Brill.

Umezu, T. (2005). *Gōshu to iu namae (The name called Gōshu)*. Tokyo: Tokyo Shoseki

Urashima Taro

"Urashima Taro" 浦島太郎 *is a Japanese folktale about a fisherman, based on a legend recorded in multiple literary works dating to the 8th century or earlier, such as the* **Nihonshoki** *(The Chronicles of Japan) and* **Man'yōshū** *(Collection of Ten Thousand Leaves).*

Once upon a time in a seaside village, there lived a fisherman named Urashima Taro. Urashima Taro was a young man with a kind heart; he went out to sea every day to go fishing to support his elderly father and mother.

One day, on his way back from the sea, Urashima Taro saw some children gathered on the beach, making a lot of noise. He saw that they had caught a small baby turtle, and that they were all tormenting it by poking it with a stick. He felt sorry for the poor baby turtle. He said to the children, "You must not torment living creatures!" and saved the baby turtle. He took it in his hand, and returned it to the water. The turtle was happy, and it popped its head and legs out of its shell and started to swim with no trouble at all, returning to the bottom of the sea.

One day, two or three years later, Urashima Taro was once again out at sea fishing when he heard a voice call out from behind him, "Mr. Urashima! Mr. Urashima!"

When he looked behind him, a big turtle was approaching the boat.

"Sir, I am the turtle that you saved. As a sign of my gratitude, I will guide you to the Dragon Palace at the bottom of the sea," the turtle said. The turtle put Urashima Taro onto its back and started swimming. When

浦島太郎

昔々、ある海辺の村に、浦島太郎という漁師が住んでいました。浦島太郎は心のやさしい若者で、毎日海へ出かけて魚をつって年老いたお父さんとお母さんを養っていました。

ある日、浦島太郎は海から帰る途中、浜で子供たちが集まって騒いでいるのを見ました。のぞいてみると、小さい亀の子を一匹つかまえて、皆で棒でつっついていじめていました。その亀の子をかわいそうだと思った浦島太郎は、

「生き物をいじめてはいけないぞ。」

と子供たちに言って、亀の子を助けてやりました。太郎が亀の子を手にのせて海の水の中に戻してやると、亀の子は喜んで甲羅から首や手足を出して、すいすいと泳ぎ始めました。そして、海の底の方へ戻って行きました。

それから二、三年たったある日のことです。浦島太郎はまた舟にのって海で魚をつっていました。すると、うしろの方で、

it dived under the blue sea a short time later, their surroundings were suddenly illuminated. They were surrounded by a coral reef, and schools of beautiful fish were swimming by. After they had been going for a while, an elegant gateway came into view in front of them. A fish led Urashima Taro into the Dragon Palace.

Inside the Dragon Palace, there was a beautiful princess.

"Welcome to the Dragon Palace. Thank you for saving the turtle the other day. Please, relax and enjoy yourself," she said with a kind voice.

After that, Urashima Taro watched the beautiful fish dance, drank sake, enjoyed wondrous feasts, merrily chatted with the princess, and lived every day like it was a dream in the Palace.

However, after a time, Urashima Taro became worried about his mother and father back in the village, and thought that he would like to return home soon. When he told this to the princess, she gave him a beautiful box to take with him, and said, "I will miss you, but it is natural for you to want to return home. This is a *tamatebako*, a treasure box. Please take it with you, and be careful returning home. But please, never open this box."

Urashima Taro took the treasure box, got onto the turtle's back, and set off towards his village.

However, when he arrived at the shore, everything around him had completely changed. There were people there as he walked towards the village, but he knew none of them. His own house in the village was gone. No matter how many times he called out to his mother and father, they couldn't be found. Urashima Taro was very shaken up.

At that moment, he suddenly caught sight of the *tamatebako*, and he gently tried to open it. When he did, white smoke came out from inside

「浦島さん、浦島さん」
と、呼ぶ声がしました。ふりかえってみますと、一匹の大きい亀が舟のそばに来ていました。
「わたくしは、前に助けていただいた亀でございます。お礼に海の底にある竜宮城にご案内いたしましょう。」
と、亀が言いました。亀は背中に浦島太郎をのせて泳ぎ出しました。青い海中をしばらく潜っていくと、急にまわりが明るくなりました。あたり一面は珊瑚礁になり、きれいな魚がたくさん泳いでいました。そして、またしばらく行くと、向こうに立派な門が見えました。魚たちは浦島太郎を竜宮城の中に案内しました。
竜宮城の中には美しい乙姫様がいて、
「ようこそ竜宮城へいらっしゃいました。先日は亀を助けてくださってありがとうございました。どうぞゆっくり遊んでいってください。」
と、やさしい声で言いました。それから、浦島太郎は竜宮城できれいな魚たちの踊りを見たり、お酒を飲んだり、すばらしいご馳走を食べたり、乙姫様と楽しくお話ししたりして、夢のような毎日を過ごしました。
ところが、しばらくすると、浦島太郎は村にいるお父さんとお母さんのことが心配になりました。そして、早くうちに帰りたいと思いました。そのことを乙姫様に言うと、乙姫様はきれいな箱を持って来てこう言いました。
「さびしくなりますが、おうちにお帰りになりたいのは当然です。これは玉手箱です。これを持って気をつけてお帰りになってください。しかし、決してこの箱を開けないでくださいね。」

it. As he silently watched the smoke, in the blink of an eye the young Urashima Taro turned into an old man with white hair and a white beard.

While he had been having fun every day in the Dragon Palace, hundreds of years had passed on land.

浦島太郎は玉手箱を持って、亀の背中にのって、村へと向かいました。

ところが、海辺に着くと、あたりの様子はすっかり変わっていました。村の方に歩いていくと人がいましたが、どの人も知らない人でした。村には自分の家はありませんでした。お父さんもお母さんもいくら呼んでも見つかりません。浦島太郎はすっかり困ってしまいました。その時、ふと玉手箱が目に入りました。そして、浦島太郎はそれをそっと開けてみました。すると、中から白い煙が出てきました。太郎がだまってその煙を見ていると、若者だった浦島太郎はたちまち白い髭と髪の老人になってしまいました。浦島太郎が竜宮城で楽しい毎日を過ごしている間に、地上では何百年も経っていたのでした。

Translator's Notes

1. There is no corresponding adverb for the mimetic word すいすい **sui-sui**, so it was paraphrased as "with no trouble at all."
2. The word **sake** is quite commonly known as "rice wine" or "alcohol" by English speakers now, so it was directly rendered to preserve the nuance of Japanese culture.
3. 玉手箱 **tamatebako** is a magical object that first appeared in this folktale, and takes the shape of a treasure box. It became widely known by Japanese through this folktale, and a proverb was later created using this word. The Japanese proverb, あけてびっくり玉手箱 **Akete bikkuri tamatebako**, literally means, "Open-and-be-shocked *tamatebako*," and it is used to express a big surprise. To preserve the nuance of this keyword, this word was directly rendered as *tamatebako* followed by an explanation.
4. The politeness of the turtle's speech was expressed by the addition of "Sir" in the beginning of his statement.

Vocabulary and Expressions

■ 昔々(むかしむかし) **mukashi mukashi** once upon a time

■ ある… **aru ...** some ...

EXAMPLE:
ある人(ひと)がここへ来(き)ました。
Aru hito ga koko e kimashita.
Some person came here.

■ 海辺(うみべ) **umibe** seashore

■ 村(むら) **mura** village

■ 浦島太郎(うらしまたろう) **Urashima Tarō** the name of the protagonist (Taro Urashima)

■ …という… **... to iu ...** ... called ...

EXAMPLE:
横浜(よこはま)という所(ところ)を知っていますか。
Yokohama to iu tokoro o shitte imasu ka.
Do you know the place called Yokohama?

■ 漁師(りょうし) **ryōshi** fisherman

■ 住(す)む **sumu** to live, to reside

EXAMPLE:
父(ちち)は東京(とうきょう)に住(す)んでいます。
Chichi wa Tōkyō ni sunde imasu.
My father lives in Tokyo.

■ 心 **kokoro** heart

■ やさしい **yasashii** kind

■ 若者 **wakamono** young person

■ 毎日 **mainichi** every day

■ 海 **umi** sea, ocean

■ 出かける **dekakeru** to go out

■ 魚をつる **sakana o tsuru** to fish

■ 年老いた **toshioita** elderly, old

■ お父さん **otō-san** father

■ お母さん **okā-san** mother

■ 養う **yashinau** to support someone for living

■ 帰る **kaeru** to go home

■ …途中 **... tochū** on the way ...

■ 浜 **hama** beach, seashore

■ 子供 **kodomo** child

■ 集まる **atsumaru** to gather

■ 騒ぐ **sawagu** to make noise

■ のぞく **nozoku** to peek

■ …と **...to** when ... [GRAMMAR]

The particle と **to** follows a verb or an adjective in the plain form, and means "when ..." if the main clause is in the past tense.

EXAMPLE:

図書館に行くと、マイクさんに会いました。

Toshokan ni iku to, Maiku-san ni aimashita.

When I went to the library, I saw Mike.

■ 小さい **chīsai** small

■ 亀 **kame** turtle

■ 亀の子 **kame-no-ko** baby turtle

■ 一匹 **ip-piki** one small animal

■ つかまえる **tsukamaeru** to catch

■ 皆で **mina de** with every one as a group

■ 棒 **bō** stick

■ つっつく **tsuttsuku** to poke

■ いじめる **ijimeru** to torment, to tease

■ かわいそうな **kawaisō na** pitiful

■ 思う **omou** to think

■ 生き物 **ikimono** living thing, creature

■ …てはいけない **... te wa ikenai** must not do ...

■ 言う **iu** to say

■ 助ける **tasukeru** to save

■ 手 **te** hand

■ のせる **noseru** to place on

■ 戻す **modosu** to return

EXAMPLE:

お金(かね)を戻(もど)しました。

Okane o modoshimashita.

(I) returned the money.

- 喜(よろこ)ぶ **yorokobu** to be delighted
- 甲羅(こうら) **kōra** the hard upper shell of a turtle
- 首(くび) **kubi** neck
- 手足(てあし) **te ashi** hands/arms and feet/legs, limbs
- 出(だ)す **dasu** to take something out
- すいすい **sui-sui** [MIMETIC] swimming smoothly
- 泳(およ)ぐ **oyogu** to swim
- …始(はじ)める **... hajimeru** to start -ing
- 底(そこ) **soko** bottom
- 戻(もど)る **modoru** to return

  EXAMPLE:

  父(ちち)が戻(もど)りました。

  Chichi ga modorimashita.

  My father returned.
- 二、三年(に、さんねん) **ni-san-nen** one or two years
- また **mata** again
- 舟(ふね) **fune** boat
- うしろ **ushiro** back
- 呼(よ)ぶ **yobu** to call out
- 声(こえ) **koe** voice
- ふりかえる **furi-kaeru** to turn around
- 大(おお)きい **ōkii** big
- そば **soba** near
- 前(まえ)に **mae ni** earlier, before
- お礼(れい)に **o-rei ni** to thank (him/her)
- 竜宮城(りゅうぐうじょう) **Ryūgūjō** the Dragon Palace (*lit., the dragon-palace castle*)
- 案内(あんない)する **annai suru** to guide
- 背中(せなか) **senaka** back
- …出(だ)す **... dasu** to start -ing
- 青(あお)い **aoi** blue
- 海中(かいちゅう) **kaichū** in the sea
- しばらく **shibaraku** for a while
- 潜(くぐ)る **kuguru** to go under
- 急(きゅう)に **kyū ni** suddenly
- まわり **mawari** surroundings
- 明(あか)るい **akarui** bright
- なる **naru** to become
- あたり **atari** vicinity, nearby
- 一面(いちめん) **ichimen** the whole surface
- 珊瑚礁(さんごしょう) **sangoshō** coral reef
- 向(む)こう **mukō** over there
- 立派(りっぱ)な **rippa na** splendid
- 門(もん) **mon** gate

- 美(うつく)しい **utsukushii** beautiful
- 乙姫様(おとひめさま) **otohime-sama** Princess Oto, Lady Otohime
- 先日(せんじつ) **senjitsu** the other day
- 遊(あそ)ぶ **asobu** to enjoy oneself
- 声(こえ) **koe** voice
- きれいな **kirei na** beautiful
- 踊(おど)り **odori** dance
- …たり **-tari** to do ... and so on [GRAMMAR] Verbs and adjectives in the **tari**-form can be created just by adding り **ri** after their **ta**-form (plain past form)

  EXAMPLES:

  食(た)べたり **tabetari** *ate*

  飲(の)んだり **nondari** *drunk*

  This form can be used to list actions and states as examples. Make sure to end the sentence with the appropriately conjugated verb する **suru**.

  EXAMPLE:

  歌(うた)ったり、踊(おど)ったりしました。

  Utattari, odottari shimashita.

  (We) sang, danced, etc.
- お酒(さけ) **o-sake** alcohol, liquor
- 飲(の)む **nomu** to drink
- ご馳走(ちそう) **gochisō** feast
- 食(た)べる **taberu** to eat
- 楽(たの)しい **tanoshii** fun, enjoyable
- お話(はな)しする **o-hanashi suru** to talk
- 夢(ゆめ) **yume** dream
- …のような **... no yō na** just like ...
- 過(す)ごす **sugosu** to spend (time)
- ところが **tokoroga** however
- 心配(しんぱい) **shinpai** worry
- 早(はや)い **hayai** early
- …たい **-tai** to want to ... [GRAMMAR] たい follows a verb in the stem form and means "to want to do ..."

  EXAMPLE:

  日本(にほん)に行(い)きたいです。

  Nihon ni iki-tai desu.

  I want to go to Japan.
- 箱(はこ) **hako** box
- さびしい **sabishii** lonely
- 当然(とうぜん) **tōzen** natural, justified
- 玉手箱(たまてばこ) **tamatebako** *tamate*-box
- 持(も)つ **motsu** to hold
- 気(き)をつける **ki o tsukeru** to be careful
- 決(けっ)して **kesshite** in no way
- 開(あ)ける **akeru** to open

- 向かう **mukau** to head towards
- 着く **tsuku** to arrive
- 様子 **yōsu** appearance, state
- すっかり **sukkari** completely
- 変わる **kawaru** to change
- 人 **hito** person
- 知る **shiru** to (get to) know
- 自分 **jibun** self
- 家 **ie** house
- いくら…ても **ikura ... te mo** no matter how ...
- 見つかる **mitsukaru** to find
- 困る **komaru** to be in trouble
- その時 **sono toki** at that time
- ふと **futo** casually, incidentally
- 目に入る **me ni hairu** to happen to see
- そっと **sotto** quietly
- 白い **shiroi** white
- 煙 **kemuri** smoke
- 出る **deru** to come out
- だまる **damaru** to be silent
- たちまち **tachimachi** in a moment
- 髭 **hige** beard, mustache
- 髪 **kami** hair
- 老人 **rōjin** old person
- 地上 **chijō** above ground
- 何百年も **nanbyaku-nen mo** hundreds of years
- 経つ **tatsu** to pass

Exercises

Select the most appropriate item in the parentheses.

1. 浦島太郎の両親は（古かったです・年老いていました）。

2. 浦島太郎は子供たちに生き物をいじめて（は・も）いけないと言いました。

3. 浦島太郎は（鳥・亀）の背中にのって竜宮城に行きました。

4. 竜宮城でご馳走を食べたり、お酒を（飲んで・飲んだり）しました。

5. しばらくすると、両親(りょうしん)のことが心配(しんぱい)になって早(はや)くうちに（帰(かえ)る・帰(かえ)り）たいと思(おも)いました。

6. 乙姫様(おとひめさま)は玉手箱(たまてばこ)を浦島太郎(うらしまたろう)にあげましたが、ぜったいに（あけないで・あけなくて）くださいと言(い)いました。

7. 村(むら)につくと、自分(じぶん)の家(いえ)はなくなっていて、知(し)っている人(ひと)は（ぜんぜん・あまり）いませんでした。

8. 玉手箱(たまてばこ)を（あける・あけて）と、白(しろ)い煙(けむり)が出(で)て来(き)ました。

9. 浦島太郎(うらしまたろう)の髭(ひげ)と（髪(かみ)・顔(かお)）はたちまち白(しろ)くなってしまいました。

10. 浦島太郎(うらしまたろう)が竜宮城(りゅうぐうじょう)で楽(たの)しい毎日(まいにち)を（過(す)ごす・過(す)ごしている）間(あいだ)に、地上(ちじょう)では何百年(なんびゃくねん)も経(た)っていたのでした。

Discussion Questions

1. What kind of person do you think Urashima Taro is? Describe him as well as you can.

2. If you were Urashima Taro, would you stay in the Dragon Palace forever?

3. Have you ever had an experience of revisiting some place, only to find it completely different than you remembered?

Yuki Onna
(Snow Woman)

"Yuki Onna" 雪女 *is a Japanese folktale about a female* yōkai *that appears on snowy nights. The legend appears to have come into being during the Muromachi period (1336–1573). It is mentioned in the* renga *(collaborative poetry) written by* Sōgi *(1421–1502), a Zen monk, which appears in* Sōgi Shokoku Monogatari *(Sogi's Tales from Many Lands).*

Once upon a time, somewhere in the north country, there lived two lumberjacks named Minokichi and Mosaku. Since Minokichi was still young, he served as an apprentice under the old Mosaku. The two always took a ferryboat across the river, to cut down trees in a distant forest.

It was a winter day. Minokichi and Mosaku had gone to the forest and were cutting down trees as always. Then, a black cloud suddenly appeared, and it started to snow. In the blink of an eye, the snow flurries turned into a terrible blizzard. The two had no choice but to stop working, and started walking home. However, upon reaching the river, they discovered that the boatman had already left, and the boat had already been tied up at the opposite bank. The two had no choice but to go into the boatman's hut on the dry river bed, where they could wait out the blizzard. There was no fire in the boatman's hut, and it was only two tatami mats wide. The two lay down on the floor, and before they knew it, they had fallen asleep.

After a little while, Minokichi woke up because he felt extremely cold. The door to the hut had been left open, and snow was fluttering in.

雪女

昔々、北国のあるところに、巳之吉と茂作という二人の木こりがいました。巳之吉はまだ若くて、老いた茂作に奉公をしていました。二人はいつも渡し舟にのって川を渡り、はなれた森へ木を切りに行っていました。

ある冬の日のことです。巳之吉と茂作はいつものように二人で森の中へ行って木を切っていました。すると、にわかに黒い雲が出て来て、雪が降り出しました。そして、あっという間にひどい吹雪になりました。二人は仕方なく仕事をやめて帰ろうと歩き出しました。しかし、川へ来ると、渡し舟の船頭はもう帰ってしまい、舟は向う岸へつないでありました。二人は仕方なく河原の船頭小屋へ入り、吹雪がやむのを待つことにしました。船頭小屋には火もなく、畳二枚ほどの板が敷いてあっただけでした。二人はその板の上に横になり、いつの間にか眠ってしまいました。

しばらくすると巳之吉はあまりに寒いので目を覚ましました。小屋の戸が開けっ放しになっていて雪が小屋の中に舞い

Minokichi immediately looked over in Mosaku's direction, and saw a woman wearing a snow-white kimono. As the woman breathed a white trail of frozen breath onto Mosaku's face, his face and hands steadily turned whiter.

Minokichi tried to let out a cry of shock, and at that, the woman came towards him. Her face was beautiful, her skin was abnormally white, and her eyes were as piercing as lightning. Minokichi tried to escape, but he couldn't move or speak. The woman stared closely at Minokichi's face; he had an uncommonly handsome face for a man from the countryside.

"I will save you. But, you must not tell anyone about what happened tonight. If you say anything, you're a dead man. You understand, right? Don't forget," the woman said, before disappearing outside into the blizzard. Minokichi immediately went over to Mosaku, and tried to wake him up. But he was as cold and hard as ice. Minokichi fainted on the spot. The next morning, when Minokichi awoke, Mosaku had died.

About a year after that, one day, when Minokichi was riding the ferryboat on his way home from the forest, a beautiful young woman with a white complexion was there. When Minokichi got off the boat, he struck up a conversation with the young woman. She had lost her parents and was in trouble, and said that she was on the way to go to the capital to look for work and a place to live. Minokichi felt bad for her, and allowed the woman to stay at his house. Her name was Oyuki. Before long, she and Minokichi were married. Oyuki took great care of Minokichi's mother, and she gave birth to ten children, one after another.

One evening, Oyuki put the children to sleep like always, and then began her needlework. As Minokichi absentmindedly stared at Oyuki's face, he remembered the woman with the white kimono who he had seen in the boatman's hut long ago.

込んでいたのです。巳之吉はとっさに茂作の方を見ました。すると、そこには真っ白い着物を着た女がいました。その女が茂作の顔へ白い息を吹きかけると、茂作の顔も手もどんどん白くなっていきました。

巳之吉は驚いて声を出そうとしました。すると、女は今度は巳之吉の方へ来ました。女の顔は美しかったですが、肌は異常に白く目は稲妻のように鋭かったです。巳之吉は逃げようとしましたが、体も動かなければ声も出ませんでした。女はその時巳之吉の顔をしげしげ見つめました。巳之吉は田舎には珍しい美しい顔をもつ若者だったのです。

「お前さんは助けてやろう。でも、今夜のことをだれにも話しちゃいけないよ。もし話したら、お前さんの命はないよ。わかったね、忘れちゃいけないよ。」

女はそう言って小屋を出て、吹雪の中へ姿を消しました。巳之吉はすぐに茂作の方へ行って起こそうとしました。しかし、茂作は氷のように冷く固くなっていました。巳之吉はその場で気を失ってしまいました。次の日の朝、巳之吉が目を覚ますと、茂吉は死んでいました。

それから一年ほど経ちました。ある日、巳之吉が森からの帰りに渡し舟に乗ると、そこにきれいな色の白い若い女がいました。巳之吉は舟を降りると、その女に話しかけました。女は両親をなくし困ってしまい、仕事と住むところを探しに都に行くところだと言いました。巳之吉は気の毒に思い、女をうちに泊めてあげました。女はお雪という名前でした。やがて、巳之吉とお雪は夫婦になりました。お雪は巳之吉の母親をひどく大事にしてあげました。そして、次々に十人の子供を産みました。

"Hey, Oyuki," he said. "A long time ago, I met a woman who was beautiful like you. Her complexion was incredibly white like yours. This was when I was staying in the boatman's hut during a blizzard. I often thought it was a dream, but because Mosaku was killed, she must have been the Snow Woman, as I suspected."

Oyuki suddenly looked at Minokichi with a terrifying look in her eyes, and said, "That woman was me. I told you not to tell anyone, but you broke your promise. Even so, I won't kill you. But in return, please take care of our children for me."

As she left him with these words, her body turned into a white mist and floated out from the small window near the ceiling.

ある晩、お雪は、いつものように子供たちを寝かせた後で、針仕事を始めました。巳之吉はぼんやりお雪の顔を見つめていると、昔、船頭小屋で見た白い着物の女のことを思い出しました。

「おい、お雪、俺は昔、お前のように美しい女に会ったことがある。お前とそっくりで、色がすごく白かった。吹雪で、船頭小屋に泊ったときだ。何度も夢かと思ったが、茂作さんが殺されたんだから、やっぱりあの女は雪女だったんだろう。」

お雪はいきなり恐ろしい目をして巳之吉を見ました。そして、こう言いました。

「あれはわたしだよ。あの時、だれにも話しちゃいけないと言ったのに、約束を破ってしまったんだね。でも、お前さんは殺さないよ。そのかわりに子供たちを可愛がってやっておくれ。」

こう言い残すと、お雪の体は白い霞のようになって、天井のそばの小さい窓から出て行ってしまいました。

Translator's Notes

1. 渡し舟 **watashi-bune** literary means crossing-boat. It is used for crossing a river in this context, and is relatively small. To give a better image to it, it was rendered as "ferryboat."
2. To express the level of informality and the bluntness in the Snow Woman's speech, もし話したら、お前さんの命はないよ **Moshi hanashitara, omae-san no inochi wa nai yo** was rendered as "if you say anything, you're a dead man."

Vocabulary and Expressions

■ 昔々 **mukashi mukashi** once upon a time

■ 北国 **kitaguni** north country

■ ある… **aru ...** some, one ...

EXAMPLE:

ある時、知らない人がうちに来ました。

Aru toki shiranai hito ga uchi ni kimashita.

A stranger came to my house one day.

■ …という… **... to iu ...** ... called ...

EXAMPLE:

べんてんというレストランを知っていますか。

Benten to iu resutoran o shitte imasu ka.

Do you know the restaurant called Benten?

■ 二人 **futari** two people

■ 木こり **kikori** woodcutter, lumberjack

■ 若い **wakai** young

■ 老いた **oita** old (for a person)

■ 年季奉公 **nenki-bōkō** apprenticeship

■ 渡し舟 **watashi-bune** a boat for crossing a river

■ 渡る **wataru** to cross

■ はなれた **hanareta** distant

■ 森 **mori** forest

■ 切る **kiru** to cut

■ …に行く **... ni iku** to go somewhere to do ... [GRAMMAR] To show the purpose of coming and going, use a verb in the stem form and the particle に.

EXAMPLE:

スーパーにバナナを買いに行きました。

Sūpā ni banana o kai ni ikimashita.

I went to a supermarket to buy bananas.

■ 冬 **fuyu** winter
■ いつものように **itsumo no yō ni** as usual
■ にわかに **niwakani** suddenly
■ 黒い **kuroi** black, dark
■ 雲 **kumo** cloud
■ 雪 **yuki** snow
■ 出て来る **dete kuru** to come out
■ 降る **furu** to fall (for rain and snow)

EXAMPLE:

雨が降りました。

Ame ga furimashita.

It rained.

■ …出す **... dasu** to start -ing abruptly

EXAMPLE:

赤ちゃんが泣き出しました。

Aka-chan ga naki-dashimashita.

A baby started to cry.

■ あっという間に **atto iu ma ni** in the blink of an eye; in the time it takes to say "Ah!"
■ ひどい **hidoi** terrible
■ 吹雪 **fubuki** snow storm, blizzard
■ 仕方なく **shikata naku** as a last resort
■ 仕事 **shigoto** work
■ やめる **yameru** to stop, to quit
■ 帰る **kaeru** to go home
■ 帰ろうと **kaerō to** trying to go home
■ 歩く **aruku** to walk
■ …と **... to** when ... [GRAMMAR]
The particle と **to** follows a verb or an adjective in the plain form, and means "when ..." if the main clause is in the past tense.

EXAMPLE:

うちに帰ると、電気がついていました。

Uchi ni kaeru to, denki ga tsuite imashita.

When I got home, the light was on.

■ 船頭 **sendō** boatman
■ …しまう **... shimau** to have

done ... [GRAMMAR] しまう is an auxiliary verb. It follows a verb in the **te**-form and shows that the action is completely done and irreversible.

EXAMPLE:

クッキーをたくさん食べてしまいました。

Kukkī o takusan tabete shimaimashita.

I have eaten a lot of cookies (and I regret it).

- 向う岸 **mukō-gishi** opposite bank
- つなぐ **tsunagu** to tie
- 河原 **kawara** dry river bed
- 船頭小屋 **sendō-goya** a boatman's hut
- 入る **hairu** to enter
- やむ **yamu** to stop
- 待つ **matsu** to wait
- …ことにする **... koto ni suru** to decide on ...

  EXAMPLE:

  数学を専攻することにしました。

  Sūgaku o senkō suru koto ni shimashita.

  I decided to major in mathematics.

- 火 **hi** fire
- 畳 **tatami** tatami mat
- 二枚 **ni-mai** two, followed by the counter for flat items
- 板 **ita** board, plank
- 敷く **shiku** to lay out
- …ある **... aru** to have ... [GRAMMAR] ある can work as an auxiliary verb following a transitive verb in the **te**-form, and expresses the state that results from the action.

  EXAMPLE:

  テレビがつけてあります。

  Terebi ga tsukete arimasu.

  The TV is turned on.

- …だけ **... dake** just ...
- 横になる **yoko ni naru** to lie down
- いつの間にか **itsu no ma ni ka** before one knows
- 眠る **nemuru** to sleep
- しばらくすると **shibaraku suru to** after a little while
- あまりに **amari ni** excessively
- 寒い **samui** cold
- …ので **... no de** because ... [GRAMMAR] ので follows a clause that specifies the reason for the

statement in the main clause.

EXAMPLE:

あしたはテストがあるので、今日は勉強します。

Ashita wa tesuto ga aru node, kyō wa benkyō shimasu.

I have a test tomorrow, so I will study today.

- 目を覚ます **me o samasu** to wake up
- 戸 **to** door
- 開けっ放し **akeppanashi** leaving open

EXAMPLE:

窓を開けっぱなしにしないでください。

Mado o akeppanashi ni shinaide kudasai.

Please don't leave the window open.

- 舞い込む **maikomu** to come fluttering in
- とっさに **tossa ni** right away
- 真っ白い **masshiroi** pure white
- 着物 **kimono** kimono
- 着る **kiru** to wear
- 顔 **kao** face
- 白い **shiroi** white
- 息 **iki** breath
- 吹きかける **fuki-kakeru** to blow upon
- どんどん **dondon** [MIMETIC] steadily
- 驚く **odoroku** to be shocked
- 声 **koe** voice
- 出す **dasu** to let something out
- …とする **... to suru** to attempt

[GRAMMAR] A verb in the volitional form can be followed by とする **to suru**, meaning "to attempt to do something."

EXAMPLE:

逃げようとしましたが、逃げられませんでした。

Nigeyō to shimashita ga, nige-raremasen deshita.

I tried to escape, but I couldn't.

- 今度 **kondo** this time
- 美しい **utsukushii** beautiful
- 肌 **hada** skin
- 異常に **ijō ni** abnormally
- 目 **me** eye
- 稲妻 **inazuma** lightning
- …のよう **... no yō** just like ...
- 鋭い **surudoi** sharp
- 逃げる **nigeru** to run away

- 体 **karada** body
- 動く **ugoku** move
- 出る **deru** to come out
- …なければ…ない **... nakereba ... nai** not ... nor ...
- その時 **sono toki** at that time
- しげしげ **shigeshige** [MIMETIC] closely
- 見つめる **mitsumeru** to gaze at, to stare at
- 田舎 **inaka** countryside
- 珍しい **mezurashii** rare
- お前さん **omae-san** you (informal, archaic)
- 助ける **tasukeru** to save (a life)
- …やる **... yaru** to do ... for you (informal version of あげる) [GRAMMAR] The verb やる means to give, but it functions as an auxiliary verb and follows a verb in the **te**-form and shows that the action is performed for the person.
- 今夜 **kon'ya** tonight
- だれにも **dare ni mo** (not) to anyone
- 話す **hanasu** to tell
- …ちゃいけない **... cha ikenai** must not ... (informal)
- もし…たら **moshi ... tara** if ...

  EXAMPLE:

  もし雨が降ったら、映画を見ます。

  Moshi ame ga futtara, eiga o mimasu.

  If it rains, I'll watch a movie.
- 命 **inochi** life
- 忘れる **wasureru** to forget
- 言う **iu** to say
- 出る **deru** to leave
- 姿を消す **sugata o kesu** to disappear
- 起こす **okosu** to wake someone up
- 氷 **kōri** ice
- 冷い **tsumetai** cold
- 固い **katai** hard
- その場で **sono ba de** on the spot
- 気を失う **ki o ushinau** to lose consciousness, to faint
- 次の日 **tsugi no hi** the next day
- 朝 **asa** morning
- 死ぬ **shinu** to die
- 一年 **ichi-nen** one year
- …ほど **... hodo** approximately
- 経つ **tatsu** to pass (time)

- …の帰りに **... no kaeri ni** on the way home
- 色 **iro** color, complexion
- 降りる **oriru** to get off
- 話しかける **hanashi-kakeru** to talk to
- 両親 **ryōshin** parents
- なくす **nakusu** to lose
- 困る **komaru** to be in trouble
- 住むところ **sumu tokoro** the place to live in
- 探す **sagasu** to look for
- 都 **miyako** capital (city)
- …ところ **... tokoro** at the moment when ...

  EXAMPLE:

  今、食べているところです。

  Ima, tabete iru tokoro desu.

  I'm in the middle of eating now.
- 気の毒に思う **ki no doku ni omou** to feel pitiful
- 泊める **tomeru** to give shelter to, to lodge
- 名前 **namae** name
- 夫婦 **fūfu** married couple
- 母親 **hahaoya** mother
- ひどく **hidoku** terribly, extremely
- 大事にする **daiji ni suru** treat (a person or a thing) seriously and with care
- 次々に **tsugitsugi ni** one after another
- 十人 **jū-nin** ten persons
- 子供を産む **kodomo o umu** to give birth to a child
- 晩 **ban** evening
- 寝かせる **nekaseru** to let someone sleep
- …後で **... ato de** after ...
- 針仕事 **hari-shigoto** needlework, sewing
- 始める **hajimeru** to start
- ぼんやり **bon'yari** vaguely absentmindedly
- 思い出す **omoi-dasu** to recall
- おい **oi** Hey!
- 俺 **ore** I or me (for male, informal)
- 会う **au** to meet
- …ことがある **... koto ga aru** to have an experience of …
- そっくり **sokkuri** exactly like
- 泊る **tomaru** to stay over ...
- 何度も **nando mo** numerous times
- 夢 **yume** dream

- 殺す **korosu** to kill
- 殺される **korosareru** to be killed
- やっぱり **yappari** as expected
- 雪女 **Yuki Onna** Snow Woman
- …だろう **... darō** probably ...
- いきなり **ikinari** abruptly
- 恐ろしい **osoroshii** terrifying, frightening, frightened
- 約束 **yakusoku** promise
- 破る **yaburu** to break
- そのかわりに **sono kawari ni** in return
- 可愛がる **kawaigaru** to love and to take care of with affection
- …おくれ **... okure** Please do ... (an archaic and informal version of ください **kudasai**)
- 言い残す **ii-nokosu** to leave word with (a person)
- 霞 **kasumi** mist
- 天井 **tenjō** ceiling
- 小さい **chīsai** small
- 窓 **mado** window
- 出て行く **dete iku** to go out

Exercises

Select the most appropriate item in the parentheses.

1. 巳之吉と茂作は毎日はなれた森へ木を（切る・切り）に行っていました。

2. ある日、巳之吉と茂作は森で吹雪（で・に）あい、船頭小屋に泊りました。

3. 船頭小屋には畳二枚くらいの板が敷いて（いて・あって）、巳之吉と茂作はそこで寝ました。

4. しばらくすると白い着物の女が茂作に（息・雪）を吹きかけて殺してしまいました。

5. 巳之吉は（動く・動こう）としましたが、動けませんでした。

6. しかし、女は巳之吉にはだれにもその晩のことを話さないように約束させて、巳之吉を助けて（やりました・もらいました）。

7. 巳之吉は一年後にきれいな色の白い若い女に渡し舟の中（に・で）会いました。

8. 巳之吉はその女と結婚して子供がたくさん（産みました・生まれました）。

9. ある日、巳之吉は妻に雪女のことを（話す・話して）しまいました。

10. すると、妻は巳之吉が約束を破ったと言って怖い顔をし、自分がその雪女だったと言って姿を消して（ありました・しまいました）。

Discussion Questions

1. Why do you think the Snow Woman chose not to kill Minokichi?

2. Why do you think the Snow Woman left her children behind?

3. Have you ever heard of or read any other scary stories related to snow?

The Spider's Thread

by Ryūnosuke Akutagawa

芥川龍之介 (AKUTAGAWA Ryūnosuke 1892–1927)
Ryūnosuke Akutagawa was born in 1892 in Tokyo. His mother developed a mental illness shortly after he was born, and he was adopted and raised by his maternal aunt and her husband. Akutagawa was sickly and hypersensitive as a boy. He studied English literature at the Tokyo Imperial University (currently the University of Tokyo) and taught English for a short time after graduation. He admired and was mentored by Sōseki Natsume. He got married to Fumi Tsukamoto in 1918 and they had three children. Akutagawa committed suicide in 1927 at the age of 35.

His representative literary works include "Rashōmon" (羅生門), "Hana" (鼻), *and* "Toshishun" (杜子春). "Kumo no Ito" (蜘蛛の糸) *was written in 1918.*

⁂ **[PART ONE]** ⁂

Once upon a time, Buddha was taking a stroll alone along the edge of the lotus pond in Paradise. All the lotus flowers blooming in the pond were as white as pearls, and an indescribably lovely scent coming from their golden stamens endlessly filled the air. It was perhaps early morning in Paradise.

Before long, Buddha paused at the edge of the pond, and from between the leaves of the lotus flowers covering the water's surface, he saw the scene below. Below the lotus pond of Paradise was the bottom of Hell; the River of Death and the Mountain of Needles could be seen clearly through the crystal-like water, like looking through a water scope.

芥川龍之介

✻✻✻ **[PART ONE]** ✻✻✻

ある日の事でございます。御釈迦様は極楽の蓮池のふちを、独りでぶらぶら御歩きになっていらっしゃいました。池の中に咲いている蓮の花は、みんな玉のようにまっ白で、そのまん中にある金色の蕊からは、何とも云えない好い匂が、絶間なくあたりへ溢れて居ります。極楽は丁度朝なのでございましょう。

やがて御釈迦様はその池のふちに御佇みになって、水の面を蔽っている蓮の葉の間から、ふと下の容子を御覧になりました。この極楽の蓮池の下は、丁度地獄の底に当って居りますから、水晶のような水を透き徹して、三途の河や針の山の景色が、丁度覗き眼鏡を見るように、はっきりと見えるのでございます。

Thereupon, amidst the other sinners, the writhing form of a man caught Buddha's eye. This man, named Kandata, was a great thief who had committed many terrible crimes, such as killing people and setting houses on fire. Yet, even he had once done a good deed. One day, as he was passing through a thick forest, he saw a small spider crawling by the road. Kandata immediately raised his foot to step on it, but he suddenly changed his mind. "No, no, even though it is small, it must have a life. How pitiful it would be to recklessly take that life," he said to himself. So finally, he helped the spider without killing it.

As Buddha looked upon this scene in Hell, he remembered the time Kandata had saved the spider. He thought that, if he could, he should save this man from Hell as a reward for this good deed. Fortunately, beside him, a spider of Paradise was spinning its silvery thread on a jade-colored lotus leaf. Buddha gently took the spider's thread in his hand, and lowered it straight down between the pearl-like white lotuses, towards Hell far below.

⁂ **[PART TWO]** ⁂

At the bottom of Hell was the Pond of Blood, and Kandata was in it trying to stay afloat amongst the other sinners. No matter where you looked,

するとその地獄の底に、犍陀多と云う男が一人、ほかの罪人と一しょに蠢いている姿が、御眼に止まりました。この犍陀多と云う男は、人を殺したり家に火をつけたり、いろいろ悪事を働いた大泥坊でございますが、それでもたった一つ、善い事を致した覚えがございます。と申しますのは、ある時この男が深い林の中を通りますと、小さな蜘蛛が一匹、路ばたを這って行くのが見えました。そこで犍陀多は早速足を挙げて、踏み殺そうと致しましたが、「いや、いや、これも小さいながら、命のあるものに違いない。その命を無暗にとると云う事は、いくら何でも可哀そうだ。」と、こう急に思い返して、とうとうその蜘蛛を殺さずに助けてやったからでございます。

御釈迦様は地獄の容子を御覧になりながら、この犍陀多には蜘蛛を助けた事があるのを御思い出しになりました。そうしてそれだけの善い事をした報には、出来るなら、この男を地獄から救い出してやろうと御考えになりました。幸い、側を見ますと、翡翠のような色をした蓮の葉の上に、極楽の蜘蛛が一匹、美しい銀色の糸をかけて居ります。御釈迦様はその蜘蛛の糸をそっと御手に御取りになって、玉のような白蓮の間から、遥か下にある地獄の底へ、まっすぐにそれを御下しなさいました。

✻✻✻ **[PART TWO]** ✻✻✻

こちらは地獄の底の血の池で、ほかの罪人と一しょに、浮いたり沈んだりしていた犍陀多でございます。何しろどちらを見ても、まっ暗で、たまにそのくら暗からぼんやり浮き上っているものがあると思いますと、それは恐ろしい針の山の針

it was completely dark, except for the faint glimmer that occasionally came from the terrifying Mountain of Needles. There was nothing else but hopelessness and despair. The whole place was as deathly silent as a graveyard; the only sound that could be heard was the occasional faint sigh of the sinners. Perhaps the humans who had fallen so deep into Hell had suffered through so much torture that they had no strength left for crying. Even the great thief Kandata could only writhe like a dying frog as he was choked by the Pond of Blood.

One day, Kandata happened to raise his head. As he gazed out into the silent darkness of the sky above the Pond of Blood, he saw the silver spider's thread descending above him smoothly in a single shimmering line, coming from the distant heavens as if it was afraid of being seen. As soon as Kandata saw this, he clapped his hands joyfully. If he could cling to this thread, and climb high enough, surely he could escape from Hell. And why stop there? If everything went smoothly, he might even be able to reach Paradise! Then, he would no longer be chased up the Mountain of Needles or drowned in the Pond of Blood.

Thinking this, Kandata immediately grasped the spider's thread firmly with both hands and started climbing it higher and higher with all his might. As he was originally a great thief, he had experience with this sort of thing.

⁂⁂⁂ [PART THREE] ⁂⁂⁂

But because so many thousands of miles separate Hell and Paradise, the ascent was not easy, no matter how fervently he climbed. After having climbed for a while, Kandata eventually grew tired and was unable to climb any farther. He had no other choice, so he paused to rest. As he

が光るのでございますから、その心細さと云ったらございません。その上あたりは墓の中のようにしんと静まり返って、たまに聞えるものと云っては、ただ罪人がつく微な嘆息ばかりでございます。これはここへ落ちて来るほどの人間は、もうさまざまな地獄の責苦に疲れはてて、泣声を出す力さえなくなっているのでございましょう。ですからさすが大泥坊の犍陀多も、やはり血の池の血に咽びながら、まるで死にかかった蛙のように、ただもがいてばかり居りました。

　ところがある時の事でございます。何気なく犍陀多が頭を挙げて、血の池の空を眺めますと、そのひっそりとした暗の中を、遠い遠い天上から、銀色の蜘蛛の糸が、まるで人目にかかるのを恐れるように、一すじ細く光りながら、するすると自分の上へ垂れて参るのではございませんか。犍陀多はこれを見ると、思わず手を拍って喜びました。この糸に縋りついて、どこまでものぼって行けば、きっと地獄からぬけ出せるのに相違ございません。いや、うまく行くと、極楽へはいる事さえも出来ましょう。そうすれば、もう針の山へ追い上げられる事もなくなれば、血の池に沈められる事もある筈はございません。

　こう思いましたからは、早速その蜘蛛の糸を両手でしっかりとつかみながら、一生懸命に上へ上へとたぐりのぼり始めました。元より大泥坊の事でございますから、こう云う事には昔から、慣れ切っているのでございます。

✻✻✻ [PART THREE] ✻✻✻

しかし地獄と極楽との間は、何万里となくございますから、いくら焦って見た所で、容易に上へは出られません。ややし

dangled from the thread, he looked into the depths below. Climbing so hard had been worth it, because the Pond of Blood where he had been not moments before had now disappeared into the darkness below. Even the faint glimmering of the terrifying Mountain of Needles was below him. If he kept climbing at this rate, escaping from Hell might be easier than he expected. Kandata wound the spider's thread around his hands, and with a voice he had not used in many years since coming here, he laughed and said "Alright, alright!" However, he suddenly noticed an innumerable number of sinners scrambling up the spider's thread after him like a line of ants, climbing higher and higher toward him unyieldingly. When Kandata saw this, he was dumbstruck with surprise and fear for a moment, watching the scene below him, his mouth hanging open like a fool. The thin spider's thread seemed like it was about to give out even with just him hanging on it, so how could it bear the weight of so many people? If it did break on his way up, he would plunge straight back into Hell, even though he had taken great pains to climb to where he was now. As he thought about how terrible that would be, the line of hundreds and thousands of sinners was diligently crawling up the thin, shining spider's thread from the dark depths of the Pond of Blood below. If he did not somehow stop them now, the thread would break in two in the middle, and there was no doubt that he would fall.

With a loud voice, Kandata shouted, "Hey, all you sinners! This spider's thread is mine! Who said you could climb up? Get off! Get off!"

It was at that moment that the spider's thread, which had shown no signs of breaking before then, suddenly snapped right where Kandata was hanging on. Even Kandata was left behind, with no hope of ever escaping. Without even having time to scream, he spun around like a top cutting through the air, plunging headfirst into the darkness below.

ばらくのぼる中に、とうとう犍陀多もくたびれて、もう一たぐりも上の方へはのぼれなくなってしまいました。そこで仕方がございませんから、まず一休み休むつもりで、糸の中途にぶら下りながら、遥かに目の下を見下しました。

すると、一生懸命にのぼった甲斐があって、さっきまで自分がいた血の池は、今ではもう暗の底にいつの間にかかくれて居ります。それからあのぼんやり光っている恐しい針の山も、足の下になってしまいました。この分でのぼって行けば、地獄からぬけ出すのも、存外わけがないかも知れません。犍陀多は両手を蜘蛛の糸にからみながら、ここへ来てから何年にも出した事のない声で、「しめた。しめた。」と笑いました。ところがふと気がつきますと、蜘蛛の糸の下の方には、数限もない罪人たちが、自分ののぼった後をつけて、まるで蟻の行列のように、やはり上へ上へ一心によじのぼって来るではございませんか。犍陀多はこれを見ると、驚いたのと恐しいのとで、しばらくはただ、莫迦のように大きな口を開いたまま、眼ばかり動かして居りました。自分一人でさえ断れそうな、この細い蜘蛛の糸が、どうしてあれだけの人数の重みに堪える事が出来ましょう。もし万一途中で断れたと致しましたら、折角ここへまでのぼって来たこの肝腎な自分までも、元の地獄へ逆落しに落ちてしまわなければなりません。そんな事があったら、大変でございます。が、そう云う中にも、罪人たちは何百となく何千となく、まっ暗な血の池の底から、うようよと這い上って、細く光っている蜘蛛の糸を、一列になりながら、せっせとのぼって参ります。今の中にどうかしなければ、糸はまん中から二つに断れて、落ちてしまうのに違いありません。

Afterwards, the only thing left hanging in the moonless and starless sky was the glimmering of the thin spider's thread from Paradise.

✻✻✻ **[PART FOUR]** ✻✻✻

Buddha was standing at the edge of the lotus pond in Paradise, steadily watching the events unfold from beginning to end. Before long, he saw Kandata sink like a stone in the Pond of Blood. He made a sad expression and resumed his strolling once again. For trying to escape from Hell, Kandata had received the divine punishment of falling back down into Hell, befitting his merciless heart. Seeing this, Buddha must have thought him a shameful creature.

However, the lotus flowers of the lotus pond of Paradise were not at all concerned about these events. These pearl-white flowers swayed gently around the feet of Buddha, and an indescribably lovely fragrance from their stamens filled the air. By then, it was perhaps nearing noon in Paradise.

そこで犍陀多は大きな声を出して、「こら、罪人ども。この蜘蛛の糸は己のものだぞ。お前たちは一体誰に尋いて、のぼって来た。下りろ。下りろ。」と喚きました。

その途端でございます。今まで何ともなかった蜘蛛の糸が、急に犍陀多のぶら下っている所から、ぷつりと音を立てて断れました。ですから犍陀多もたまりません。あっと云う間もなく風を切って、独楽のようにくるくるまわりながら、見る見る中に暗の底へ、まっさかさまに落ちてしまいました。

後にはただ極楽の蜘蛛の糸が、きらきらと細く光りながら、月も星もない空の中途に、短く垂れているばかりでございます。

＊＊＊ [PART FOUR] ＊＊＊

御釈迦様は極楽の蓮池のふちに立って、この一部始終をじっと見ていらっしゃいましたが、やがて犍陀多が血の池の底へ石のように沈んでしまいますと、悲しそうな御顔をなさりながら、またぶらぶら御歩きになり始めました。自分ばかり地獄からぬけ出そうとする、犍陀多の無慈悲な心が、そうしてその心相当な罰をうけて、元の地獄へ落ちてしまったのが、御釈迦様の御目から見ると、浅間しく思召されたのでございましょう。

しかし極楽の蓮池の蓮は、少しもそんな事には頓着致しません。その玉のような白い花は、御釈迦様の御足のまわりに、ゆらゆら萼を動かして、そのまん中にある金色の蕊からは、何とも云えない好い匂が、絶間なくあたりへ溢れて居ります。極楽ももう午に近くなったのでございましょう。

✻✻✻ [LESSON FOR PART ONE] ✻✻✻

Translator's Notes

1. It is difficult to express the same level of politeness toward Buddha in English due to the lack of honorific expressions that correspond to the prefix 御 **go** or polite verbs like ございます **gozaimasu** in Japanese.
2. Specific terms from Buddhism such as 極楽 **gokuraku** and 三途の川 **sanzu-no-kawa** are also a part of commonly held concepts in Japan. These words are translated following Eugene Nida's (1964) *Dynamic Equivalence*, where "the relationship between the receptors and the message should be substantially the same as that which existed between the original receptors and the message."
3. There is no corresponding English word for 覗き眼鏡 **nozoki-megane**, so a new word, "water scope," was created and used in this translation.

Vocabulary and Expressions

- ■ ある日 **aruhi** once upon a time
- ■ …でございます **de gozaimasu** polite version of …です **... desu**
- ■ 御釈迦様 **oshaka-sama** Buddha
- ■ 極楽 **gokuraku** Sukhavati (Amitabha's Pure Land)
- ■ 蓮 **hasu** lotus
- ■ ふち **fuchi** surrounding edge
- ■ ぶらぶら **burabura** [MIMETIC] strolling
- ■ 御…（お or ご…） **o-** or **go-** an honorific prefix used before a noun, verb, or adjective. When used before a verb in the stem form along with the particle に **ni** and the verb なる **naru** as in お歩きになる **o-aruki ni naru** or along with なさる **nasaru** as in お歩きなさる **o-aruki nasaru**, it shows respect to the performer of the action.
- ■ 玉 **tama** jewel, gem, pearl
- ■ …のように **... no yō ni** like ... [GRAMMAR] …のような **... no yō na** follows a noun and creates a **na**-type adjective that expresses a simile. To use it as an adverb,

change な to に.

EXAMPLE:

よう子さんは天使のようにやさしい人です。

Yōko-san wa tenshi no yō ni yasashii hito desu.

Yoko is a person who is kind just like an angel.

- 蕊 **zui** stamen (of a flower)
- 何とも云えない **nan to mo ienai** indescribable
- 絶え間なく **taemanaku** constantly
- あたり **atari** nearby area
- 溢れる **afureru** to overflow, to flood
- …なのでございましょう **... nano de gozaimashō** = …なのでしょう **... nano deshō** It is probably ...
- 佇む **tatazumu** to stand still
- 面 **omote** surface
- 蔽う **ōu** to cover, to conceal
- 葉 **ha** leaves
- 容子 = 様子 **yōsu** state
- 地獄 **jigoku** Hell
- 底 **soko** bottom
- 当たる **ataru** to be equivalent to
- 水晶 **suishō** crystal
- 透き徹す = 透き通す **sukitōsu** to see through
- 三途の河 **sanzu-no-kawa** Sanzu River (Buddhist equivalent of the River Styx)
- 針 **hari** needle
- 景色 **keshiki** scenery
- 覗き眼鏡 **nozoki megane** a box with a glass bottom for viewing underwater
- 罪人 **zainin** sinners
- 蠢く **ugomeku** to squirm, to writhe
- 姿 **sugata** appearance
- 眼に止まる **me ni tomaru** to catch one's eye
- …たり **-tari** do ..., etc. [GRAMMAR] Verbs and adjectives in the たり **tari**-form can be created just by adding り after their **ta**-form (plain past form). The **tari**-form can be used to list actions and states as examples. Make sure to end the sentence with the appropriately conjugated verb する **suru**.

EXAMPLE:

食べたり飲んだりしました。

Tabetari nondari shimashita.

We ate, drink, etc.

- ■ 悪事 **akuji** evil deed, crime
- ■ それでも **soredemo** even so
- ■ 致す **itasu** the humble version of する **suru**
- ■ … 覚えがある **oboe ga aru** to have done ..., to remember to have done ...
- ■ 路ばた **robata** roadside
- ■ 這う **hau** to crawl
- ■ 早速 **sassoku** immediately
- ■ 挙げる (= 上げる , あげる) **ageru** to raise
- ■ 踏む **fumu** to step on
- ■ 踏み殺す **fumi-korosu** to step on something and kill it [GRAMMAR] Using a stem form, you can create a verbal compound.

EXAMPLE:

食べすぎました。

Tabesugimashita.

I overate.

- ■ … とする **... to suru** to try to ... [GRAMMAR] とする follows a verb in the volitional form to express an attempt, which is usually not realized.

EXAMPLE:

死のうとしました。

Shinō to shimashita.

I tried to kill myself.

- ■ 小さいながら **chīsai nagara** although it is small
- ■ 命 **inochi** life
- ■ 無暗に **muyami ni** thoughtlessly, indiscriminately, recklessly
- ■ いくら何でも **ikura nan demo** whatever the circumstances may be
- ■ 思い返す **omoikaesu** to rethink, to change one's mind
- ■ 殺さずに **korosazu ni** = 殺さないで **korosanai de**
- ■ 助ける **tasukeru** to save
- ■ …やる **yaru** to ... for ... [GRAMMAR] Verbs of giving such as やる , あげる , and さしあげる can be added at the end of a verb in the **te**-form to show who the action was performed for.

EXAMPLE:

弟に本を読んであげました。

Otōto ni hon o yonde agemashita.

I read a book to my little brother.

■ 御覧になりながら **goran ni nari-nagara** while watching ... (respectful form)
■ 思い出す **omoidasu** to recall
■ 報 = 報い **mukui** reward
■ 出来るなら **dekirunara** if possible
■ 救い出す **sukuidasu** to rescue
■ 幸い **saiwai** fortunately
■ 翡翠 **hisui** jade
■ 遥か **haruka** far away

Exercises

Select the most appropriate item in the parentheses.

1. ある日、お釈迦様は極楽の（山・蓮池）のまわりを歩いていらっしゃいました。

2. 池の中に咲いている蓮の花は玉の（ような・ように）きれいでした。

3. 蓮の葉の間から下の（天国・地獄）の様子をご覧になると、犍陀多という男が見えました。

4. 犍陀多は人を殺したり家に火を（つけたり・つける）した大泥棒です。

5. でも、犍陀多は生きているときにたった一つ（いい・わるい）事をしました。

6. 生きているときに蜘蛛を殺そうとしましたが、殺さないで助けて（やり・もらい）ました。

7. お釈迦様(しゃかさま)はそのことをお思(おも)い出(だ)しになって、犍陀多を助(たす)けて（あげる・くれる）ことにしました。

8. お釈迦様(しゃかさま)のそばには極楽(ごくらく)の蜘蛛(くも)が一匹(いっぴき)、美(うつく)しい（銀色(ぎんいろ)・金色(きんいろ)）の糸(いと)をかけていました。

9. お釈迦様(しゃかさま)はその蜘蛛(くも)の糸(いと)を地獄(じごく)の底(そこ)へまっすぐお下(おろ)し（ました・なさいました）。

Discussion Questions

1. Find some background information about Akutagawa Ryūnosuke and discuss it.

2. Have you ever seen lotuses? How are lotuses described in this story?

3. Why did Buddha lower the spider's thread?

⁂ [LESSON FOR PART TWO] ⁂

Vocabulary and Expressions

- 血(ち) **chi** blood
- 浮(う)く **uku** to float
- 沈(しず)む **shizumu** to sink
- 何(なに)しろ **nanishiro** at any rate
- どちらを見(み)ても **dochira o mite mo** no matter where he looked

  [GRAMMAR] A verb or an adjective in the **te**-form followed by the particle も expresses a concession. If it includes a question word, it means "no matter ..."

  EXAMPLE:

  何(なに)を食(た)べても太(ふと)りません。
  Nani o tabete mo futorimasen.
  No matter what he eats, he doesn't gain weight.
- くら暗(くら)＝暗闇(くらやみ) **kurayami** darkness

- ■ ぼんやり **bonyari** vaguely
- ■ 浮き上る **ukiagaru** to rise to the surface
- ■ 針 **hari** needle
- ■ 光る **hikaru** to shine
- ■ 心細さ **kokoro-bososa** helplessness
- ■ …と云ったらない **... to ittara nai** nothing more ... than this; as ... as it could possibly be
- ■ 墓 **haka** tomb, gravesite
- ■ しんと **sin to** [MIMETIC] quietness
- ■ 静まり返る **shizumari-kaeru** to fall silent
- ■ 微な = 微かな **kasuka na** faint, weak
- ■ 嘆息 **tansoku** sigh
- ■ 責め苦 **semeku** torture
- ■ 疲れはてる **tsukarehateru** to get tired out
- ■ 泣声 **nakigoe** cry (*lit., crying voice*)
- ■ …さえ **... sae** even ...
- ■ さすが **sasuga** highly known and expected
- ■ やはり **yahari** expectedly
- ■ 咽ぶ **musebu** to be smothered
- ■ … ながら **... nagara** while ...
  [GRAMMAR] ながら can follow a verb in the stem form and expresses an accompanying activity.
  EXAMPLE:
  テレビを見ながら朝ごはんを食べました。
  Terebi o mi-nagara asa-gohan o tabemashita.
  I had my breakfast while watching TV.
- ■ 死にかかる **shini kakaru** to be dying
- ■ 蛙（かわず **kawazu**, かえる **kaeru**） frog
- ■ もがく **mogaku** to struggle, to writhe
- ■ …てばかりいる **-te-bakari iru** to do nothing but ... [GRAMMAR] ばかり in …ている **-te-iru** construction expresses an excessive behavior.
  EXAMPLE:
  兄はねてばかりいます。
  Ani wa nete-bakari imasu.
  My big brother does nothing but sleep.

- 何気なく **nanige-naku** unintentionally
- 頭 **atama** head
- 挙げる = 上げる **ageru** to raise
- 眺める **nagameru** to gaze
- ひっそりとした **hissori to shita** quiet, still
- 天上 **tenjō** heaven
- 銀色 **gin'iro** silver
- 人目にかかる **hitome ni kakaru** to be visible
- 恐れる **osoreru** to fear
- 一すじ **hitosuji** a string of ...
- 細い **hosoi** thin
- するすると **surusuru to** [MIMETIC] smoothly, swiftly
- 垂れる **tareru** to hang
- 参る **mairu** a humble version of 来る **kuru**
- ... と **to** then [GRAMMAR] と can connect two events that took place in the past. In this case, the same person should not have full control over both of the two events.

  EXAMPLE:

  カフェテリアに行くと、田中さんが待っていました。

  Kafeteria ni iku to, Tanaka-san ga matteimashita.

  When I went to the cafeteria, Mr. Tanaka was waiting for me.
- 思わず **omowazu** unintentionally, spontaneously
- 拍つ **utsu** to clap
- 縋りつく **sugaritsuku** to cling to
- ... ば **-ba** if ... [GRAMMAR] A verb or an adjective in the **ba**-form expresses a condition.

  EXAMPLE:

  これを飲めば、すっきりしますよ。

  Kore o nome-ba, sukkiri shimasu yo.

  If you drink this, you'll feel refreshed.
- ぬけ出す **nukedasu** to sneak away
- 相違ない **sōinai** no doubt (about it)
- 追う **ou** to chase
- 沈める **shizumeru** to submerge
- …筈はない **... hazu wa nai** ... is logically impossible
- たぐる **taguru** to pull in (rope)
- つかむ **tsukamu** to grasp, to hold
- 元より **motoyori** originally

■ 慣れる **nareru** to get used to　　■ …切る **... kiru** to do ... completely

Exercises

Select the most appropriate item in the parentheses.

1. 犍陀多は血の池で他の罪人といっしょに浮いたり、（沈んだり・やすんだり）していました。

2. 何しろ（どちら・いつ・だれ）を見てもまっ暗でした。

3. たまに恐ろしい針の山の（かたな・針・血）が光っていました。

4. そこは（墓・池）の中のようにしいんと静まり返っていました。

5. そこの人間は泣声を出す力（だけ・さえ・しか）なくなっているのでしょう。

6. 犍陀多は血の池の（血・けむり）に咽んでいました。

7. 死にかかった蛙のようにもがいて（ばかり・しか）いました。

8. ある時、天上から蜘蛛の（くさり・糸・なわ）が自分の方へ垂れて来ました。

9. その蜘蛛の糸を（見た・見る）と、犍陀多はたいへん喜びました。

10. その糸にすがりついてのぼって（行けば・行くのに）、地獄からぬけ出せるはずです。

11. 蜘蛛の糸を両手でしっかり（つかむ・つかみ）ながら、上へ上へとのぼりはじめました。

Discussion Questions

1. How is Hell described in this story?

2. What kind of images did you have about Hell before reading this story?

3. How is the spider's thread described in this story? Can it metaphorically symbolize something in our world?

✻✻✻ [LESSON FOR PART THREE] ✻✻✻

Translator's Notes

Measurement units are culture-specific. 里 (**ri**) is an old measurement for distance, approximately 3.927 km or 2.44 miles. However, 里 **ri** was rendered as "miles" in this story because the exact distance is not essential in this story and the ease of accessibility for the target audience is more important in this case.

Vocabulary and Expressions

- 中途 **chūto** in the middle
- ぶら下る **burasagaru** to dangle, to hang
- 遥か **haruka** far
- 見下す **miorosu** to look down
- すると **suru to** = そうすると **sō suru to** then
- 甲斐がある **kai ga aru** to be worthwhile
- いつの間にか **itsu-no-ma ni ka** before one knows
- かくれる **kakureru** to hide
- 恐ろしい **osoroshii** scary
- この分で **kono bun de** judging from the present situation

- 存外（ぞんがい） **zongai** contrary to expectations
- わけがない **wake ga nai** easy, simple
- からむ **karamu** to entangle
- しめた **shimeta** I've got it! Alright!
- ふと **futo** unintentionally, incidentally
- 数限（かずかぎ）りない **kazu-kagiri nai** innumerable
- 後（あと）をつける **ato o tsukeru** to follow
- 蟻（あり）の行列（ぎょうれつ） **ari no gyōretsu** line of ants
- よじのぼる **yojinoboru** to climb/clamber up
- 一心（いっしん）に **isshin ni** single-mindedly
- 驚（おどろ）く **odoroku** to be shocked, surprised
- …まま **... mama** while keeping ... [GRAMMAR] まま follows a verb in the plain past form, an adjective in the pre-nominal form, a noun followed by の or a demonstrative adjective, and expresses a situation where the same state is maintained.

EXAMPLES:

ドアを開けたまま出かけました。

Doa o aketa-mama dekake-mashita.

(He) went out, leaving the door open.

そのままにしてください。

Sonomama ni shitekudasai.

Please leave it as it is.

- 細（ほそ）い **hosoi** skinny, thin
- 人数（にんずう） **ninzū** the number of people
- 重（おも）み **omomi** weight
- 堪（た）える **taeru** to bear
- 万一（まんいち） **man'ichi** by some chance
- 途中（とちゅう）で **tochū de** in the middle
- …たら **tara** if ..., when ..., whenever ... [GRAMMAR] Verbs and adjectives in the **tara**-form can be created by adding ら **ra** after their **ta**-form (plain past form) and they can express conditions.

EXAMPLE:

田中（たなか）さんが来（き）たら、私（わたし）は帰（かえ）ります。

Tanaka-san ga kitara, watashi wa kaerimasu.

If Mr. Tanaka comes, I will go home.

■ 折角 **sekkaku** at great pains, with trouble

■ 肝腎な = 肝心な **kanjin na** essential, main

■ 逆落とし **sakaotoshi** plunging down with headfirst

■ 落ちる **ochiru** to fall

■ うようよと **uyouyo to** [MIMETIC] in swarms

■ 一列 **ichi-retsu** one line

■ 這い上がる **haiagaru** to creep/crawl up

■ せっせと **sesseto** diligently

■ 今の中に **ima no uchi ni** now, immediately

■ …ども **... domo** plural suffix (derogatory form)

EXAMPLE:

泥棒ども **dorobō-domo** *thieves*

■ お前 **omae** you (derogatory form)

■ …と **... to** quotation particle [GRAMMAR] The particle と functions as a quotation particle following either a direct quote or an indirect quote.

EXAMPLES:

「ありがとう。」と言いました。

"Arigatō" to iimashita

(I) said, "Thanks."

田中さんは去年シンガポールに行ったと言っていました。

Tanaka-san wa kyonen Shingapōru ni itta to itteimashita.

Mr. Tanaka was saying that he went to Singapore last year.

■ 喚く **wameku** to shout

■ その途端 **sono totan** at that moment

■ ぷつり **putsuri** [MIMETIC] breaking off or snapping off

■ たまらない **tamaranai** unendurable

■ …しまう **... shimau** to have done ... [GRAMMAR] しまう can follow a verb in the **te**-form and shows that the action is completely done and irreversible.

EXAMPLE:

貯金を全部使ってしまいました。

Chokin o zenbu tsukatte-shimaimashita.

I used up all of my savings.

■ あっと云う間もなく **atto iu ma mo naku** instantly (*lit., even without a moment to say "Ah"*)

■ 独楽 **koma** spinning top

■ まっさかさま **massakasama** headfirst

Exercises

Select the most appropriate item in the parentheses.

1. 極楽と（天上・地獄）との間は何万里もあります。

2. しかし、犍陀多が一生懸命のぼった（事・甲斐）があって血の池はずっと下になりました。

3. ところが、ふと気がつく（で・と）、たくさんの罪人が後からのぼってきました。

4. まるで（蟻・蜂）の行列のように上へ上へと一心にのぼってきました。

5. 犍陀多はしばらく口を（あく・あいて・あいた）まま見ていました。

6. この（細い・ふとい）蜘蛛の糸がどうしてあれだけの罪人の重みにたえることができるでしょうか。

7. もし途中で糸が（きれ・きる）たら、自分も落ちてしまうでしょう。

8. 犍陀多は「こら、罪人ども。この蜘蛛の糸はおれのものだぞ。下りろ。」（と・で）わめきました。

9. その途端に糸が（ぷつりと・くるりと）音を立ててきれました。

10. 犍陀多はあっという間にくるくるまわりながら落ちて（おき・しまい）ました。

Discussion Questions

1. What do you think Kandata was thinking when he saw so many sinners climbing up the thread?

2. How do you feel about Kandata telling the other sinners to get off? Are there people who are like him in our society?

3. Why do you think the spider's thread broke right after Kandata asked the other sinners to get off?

✻✻✻ [LESSON FOR PART FOUR] ✻✻✻

Vocabulary and Expressions

■ 一部始終 **ichibu-shijū** from beginning to end

■ 石 **ishi** stone

■ …そう **-sō** looks ... [GRAMMAR]

そう follows a verb or an adjective in the stem form and creates a **na**-type adjective that means "to be about ..." or "to look ..."

EXAMPLES:

こわれそうな車 **kowaresō na kuruma** *a car that is about to break down*

高そうなドレス **takasō na doresu** *a dress that looks expensive*

■ …ばかり **bakari** only

■ 無慈悲な **mujihi na** merciless, ruthless

■ 心 **kokoro** heart, mind, spirit

■ 相当な **sōtō na** equivalent

■ 罰 **batsu** punishment

■ うける **ukeru** to receive

■ 浅間しい **asamashii** shameful, mean, despicable

- 思召す **oboshimesu** to think (respectful form)
- 頓着する **tonjaku suru** to be mindful
- ゆらゆら **yurayura** [MIMETIC] slow swaying
- 萼（うてな **utena** = がく **gaku**） sepal
- 午 = 昼 **hiru** noon

Exercises

Select the most appropriate item in the parentheses.

1. お釈迦様は一部（始終・全部）をじっと見ていらっしゃいました。
2. 犍陀多は石のように血の池の底に（沈んで・沈み）しまいました。
3. そうすると、お釈迦様は（悲しい・悲し）そうなお顔をなさりながら、またぶらぶらお歩きはじめました。
4. お釈迦様は犍陀多の無慈悲な心と、その心相当な罰をうけて（地獄・極楽）に落ちてしまったのがあさましくお思いになりました。
5. 蓮池の（蓮・罪人）はそんな事は気にしません。
6. 極楽はいつもと同じように玉のような白い蓮の花のいい香り（を・で）いっぱいです。

Discussion Questions

1. Why did Buddha look sad?
2. What kind of lessons do you think this story teaches us? List as many as you can.

The Siblings Who Almost Drowned

by Takeo Arishima

有島武郎 (ARISHIMA Takeo 1878–1923)
Takeo Arishima was born in 1878 in Tokyo, the son of a high ranking official in the Finance Ministry of Japan. He studied at Sapporo Agricultural College, Haverford College, and Harvard University. He was once a Christian, but gradually drifted to socialism. Arishima got married to Yasuko Kamio in 1910 and they had three children. However, Yasuko died of tuberculosis in 1916. Arishima later had an affair with a married woman, Akiko Hatano, who was an editor for a literary magazine. They committed suicide together in 1923.
Arishima's representative literary works include "Aru Onna" (或る女), "Kain no Matsuei" (カインの末裔) *and* "Oshiminaku Ai wa Ubau" (惜みなく愛は奪ふ). "Oborekaketa Kyōdai" (溺れかけた兄妹) *was published in 1921.*

*** **[PART ONE]** ***

During the *doyo* season, when tall waves called "*doyo* waves" crash against the coast even in the absence of wind, people from the cities who came to swim in the sea close up their villas one by one and return home. Until then, many people would always gather on the sand and in the water, from morning till night. If you looked down from a place like on top of the sand dunes, you would wonder where such a large crowd had come from. However, by the time September had come and the third day of the month had arrived, there was no longer a soul anywhere on the beach.

My friend M, my little sister, and I decided to go swimming so that we could appreciate the last moment that we could be in the sea, and try to hang onto the last vestiges of summer. My grandmother told us that it

溺れかけた兄妹

有島武郎

✻✻✻ [PART ONE] ✻✻✻

土用波という高い波が風もないのに海岸に打寄せる頃になると、海水浴に来ている都の人たちも段々別荘をしめて帰ってゆくようになります。今までは海岸の砂の上にも水の中にも、朝から晩まで、沢山の人が集って来て、砂山からでも見ていると、あんなに大勢な人間が一たい何所から出て来たのだろうと不思議に思えるほどですが、九月にはいってから三日目になるその日には、見わたすかぎり砂浜の何所にも人っ子一人いませんでした。

私の友達のMと私と妹とはお名残だといって海水浴にゆくことにしました。お婆様が波が荒くなって来るから行かない方がよくはないかと仰有ったのですけれども、こんなにお天気はいいし、風はなしするから大丈夫だといって仰有ることを聞かずに出かけました。

would be better not to go out, because the waves had gotten rough. But the weather was so nice, and there was no wind at all, so we told her that it was okay, and we headed out without heeding her warning.

It was just past noon and the weather was fair, with not a cloud in the sky. Even though it was daytime, bugs were already chirping in the grass; nevertheless, we sometimes had to run on the grass since the sand was so hot against our bare feet. M was wearing a towel on his head and hurdling towards the water. I ran while pulling my little sister—who was wearing a straw hat—by the hand. We wanted to get to the sea as soon as possible, so the three of us hurried along breathlessly.

*** [PART TWO] ***

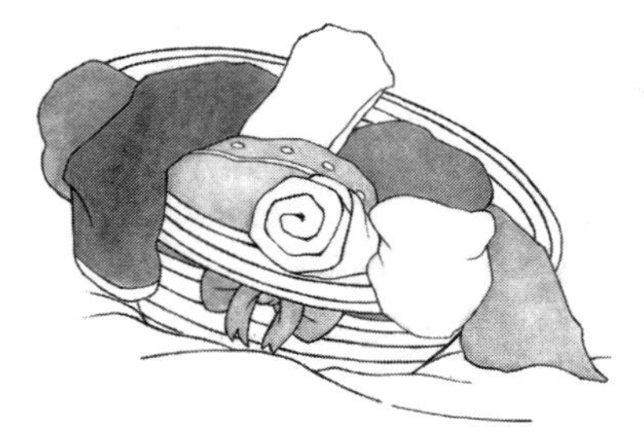

They're called "swells", right? Those kinds of waves were heaving up and down out at sea. They weren't small waves that broke on the shore with a crash, but hill-like waves that were formed farther out at sea, and gradually headed towards the shore. Before long, a crest formed on top of the wave, and it broke with a loud splash all at once. A little while after that, another hill-like wave started heading towards the shore. The wave that collapsed crashed on the sand with a huge force, and white foam sprayed everywhere. The three of us had a bit of a bad feeling, seeing the looks of the waves, but it had taken us a lot of trouble to get there, so we didn't

丁度昼少し過ぎで、上天気で、空には雲一つありませんでした。昼間でも草の中にはもう虫の音がしていましたが、それでも砂は熱くって、裸足だと時々草の上に駈け上らなければいられないほどでした。Mはタオルを頭からかぶってどんどん飛んで行きました。私は麦稈帽子を被った妹の手を引いてあとから駈けました。少しでも早く海の中につかりたいので三人は気息を切って急いだのです。

✻✻✻ **[PART TWO]** ✻✻✻

紆波といいますね、その波がうっていました。ちゃぷりちゃぷりと小さな波が波打際でくだけるのではなく、少し沖の方に細長い小山のような波が出来て、それが陸の方を向いて段々押寄せて来ると、やがてその小山のてっぺんが尖って来て、ざぶりと大きな音をたてて一度に崩れかかるのです。そうすると暫らく間をおいてまたあとの波が小山のように打寄せて来ます。そして崩れた波はひどい勢いで砂の上に這い上って、そこら中を白い泡で敷きつめたようにしてしまうのです。三人はそうした波の様子を見ると少し気味悪くも思いました。けれども折角そこまで来ていながら、そのまま引返すのはどうしてもいやでした。で、妹に帽子を脱がせて、それを砂の上に仰向けにおいて、衣物やタオルをその中に丸めこむと私たち三人は手をつなぎ合せて水の中にはいってゆきました。

「ひきがしどいね」

とMがいいました。本当にその通りでした。ひきとは水が沖の方に退いて行く時の力のことです。それがその日は大変強いように私たちは思ったのです。踝くらいまでより水の

want to go back. I had my little sister take off her hat and place it face up on the sand, and we rolled up our clothes and towels inside of it. Then, holding each other's hands, we began to move into the water.

"The pull is pretty strong," M said.

It really was just as he said. The "pull" is the strength of the receding water that was tugging us out to sea. We thought it seemed especially strong that day. Even though we were standing where the water only came up to our ankles, the water retreated like a raging river, so much so that we would have fallen down if we were not paying attention, as the sand under our feet was being pulled along with it. When we watched the water retreating out into the open sea, we felt dizzy. At the same time, it was quite captivating to us. The way that the sand was sucked away, tickling the bottom of our feet as they steadily sunk deeper and deeper, was especially amusing to us. Still holding hands, the three of us went out deeper, little by little. When we stood facing the open sea, the water pelted against the backs of our knees, and it was hard to keep our legs straight. When we faced the shore, the water hit our shins with so much force that it was painful. We stood straight with our legs together; the winner of the game would be whoever didn't fall, and we also made a game out of standing on one leg. The three of us splashed around like mermaids having fun.

While we were doing that, M tried going deeper, up to where the water came up to his knees. Having done that, each time the waves came, M had to stand on his tip toes. This again seemed fun, so we also gradually went deeper to join him. And when there were no waves, we eventually went out to where the water came up to our waists. When we went that far, simply standing up was not enough to avoid a wave when one came in. Unless we floated up, we would end up swallowing water.

来ない所に立っていても、その水が退いてゆく時にはまるで急な河の流れのようで、足の下の砂がどんどん掘れるものでですから、うっかりしていると倒れそうになる位でした。その水の沖の方に動くのを見ていると眼がふらふらしました。けれどもそれが私たちには面白くってならなかったのです。足の裏をくすむるように砂が掘れて足がどんどん深く埋まってゆくのがこの上なく面白かったのです。三人は手をつないだまま少しずつ深い方にはいってゆきました。沖の方を向いて立っていると、膝の所で足がくの字に曲りそうになります。陸の方を向いていると向脛にあたる水が痛い位でした。両足を揃えて真直に立ったままどっちにも倒れないのを勝にして見たり、片足で立ちっこをして見たりして、三人は面白がって人魚のように跳ね廻りました。

その中にMが膝位の深さの所まで行って見ました。そうすると紆波が来る度ごとにMは脊延びをしなければならないほどでした。それがまた面白そうなので私たちも段々深味に進んでゆきました。そして私たちはとうとう波のない時には腰位まで水につかるほどの深味に出てしまいました。そこまで行くと波が来たらただ立っていたままでは追付きません。どうしてもふわりと浮き上らなければ水を呑ませられてしまうのです。

✻✻✻ **[PART THREE]** ✻✻✻

ふわりと浮上ると私たちは大変高い所に来たように思いました。波が行ってしまうので地面に足をつけると海岸の方を見ても海岸は見えずに波の脊中だけが見えるのでした。その中にその波がざぶんとくだけます。波打際が一面に白くなっ

When we floated up, it felt like we went very high. After the wave went by, we put our feet on the ground, but we couldn't see the beach past the back of the wave even though we were facing the shore. The wave eventually broke with a splash. The whole surface of the beach turned white, and for an instant, we could clearly see the sand dunes and my little sister's hat. This was also extremely interesting. The three of us had completely forgotten the warning about how dangerous these *doyo* waves could be, and we continued to play our game, jumping among the waves.

"Oh, a big wave is coming!" my little sister said suddenly. She sounded frightened as she looked out into the open sea. Hearing this, we also instinctively looked that way, and it was exactly as she had said—a wave bigger than any of the others was surging forward, so big that it looked like someone who was spreading his arms wide. Even M, who was good at swimming, seemed a bit shaken, so he tried to go towards the shore and make his way towards the shallow parts, even if he could go only a little farther. It goes without saying that we followed suit. We dove forward in a swimming-like position and tried to walk while using both our hands to push through the water. But the pull was so strong that our legs were swept out from under us, and we couldn't go any farther. We felt like we were in a dream, being chased by a villain.

The wave that was closing in from behind wasn't waiting for us to reach the shallow parts. It got bigger and grew closer in the blink of an eye, and we could just see the white bubbles starting to break at the top of it. "It's no good if you keep going that way!" M cried in a loud voice from behind us.

"You'll get caught in the wave when it breaks! It's better if you go over the wave while you still have time!" he said. That seemed to be right. My

て、いきなり砂山や妹の帽子などが手に取るように見えます。それがまたこの上なく面白かったのです。私たち三人は土用波があぶないということも何も忘れてしまって波越しの遊びを続けさまにやっていました。

「あら大きな波が来てよ」

と沖の方を見ていた妹が少し怖そうな声でこういきなりいいましたので、私たちも思わずその方を見ると、妹の言葉通りに、これまでのとはかけはなれて大きな波が、両手をひろげるような恰好で押寄せて来るのでした。泳ぎの上手なMも少し気味悪そうに陸の方を向いていくらかでも浅い所まで遁げようとした位でした。私たちはいうまでもありません。腰から上をのめるように前に出して、両手をまたその前に突出して泳ぐような恰好をしながら歩こうとしたのですが、何しろひきがひどいので、足を上げることも前にやることも思うようには出来ません。私たちはまるで夢の中で怖い奴に追いかけられている時のような気がしました。

後から押寄せて来る波は私たちが浅い所まで行くのを待ってはいてくれません。見る見る大きく近くなって来て、そのてっぺんにはちらりちらりと白い泡がくだけ始めました。Mは後から大声をあげて、

「そんなにそっちへ行くと駄目だよ、波がくだけると捲きこまれるよ。今の中に波を越す方がいいよ」

といいました。そういわれればそうです。私と妹とは立止って仕方なく波の来るのを待っていました。高い波が屏風を立てつらねたように押寄せて来ました。私たち三人は丁度具合よくくだけない中に波の脊を越すことが出来ました。私たちは体をもまれるように感じながらもうまくその大波をやりすごすことだけは出来たのでした。三人はようやく安心して

little sister and I stopped and looked helplessly at the approaching wave, waiting for it to come. The tall wave was moving towards us like a line of standing folding screens. The three of us were at just the right position that we would be able to ride the wave and let it pass just before it broke. Even though we felt as though our bodies were being pummeled, we were just able to skillfully let the surging wave go past us. The three of us were very relieved, and we grinned at each other as we swam. And when the wave was gone, the three of us stopped swimming and tried to stand on the sand underneath us.

But instead, when we stopped swimming, all three of us plunged under the water together. Even though we were almost completely underwater, our feet still couldn't touch the sand. We were startled and panicked. We paddled and thrashed around as hard as we could, and finally we managed to get our faces above the water. We exchanged glances, our expressions incredulous. Our faces and lips were a bluish pale, and our eyes looked like they were about to fall out of our heads. Even though we didn't say anything to each other, we all knew that we had been instantly carried somewhere very deep just by that one wave. We looked towards the shore and understood that we had to swim back as fast as we could.

⁂ [PART FOUR] ⁂

We silently started swimming on our sides. But, please try to consider how much strength we had left. M was fourteen. I was thirteen. My younger sister was eleven. Since M was in the swimming club every year at school, he naturally knew how to swim; I had just learned how to do the sidestroke and how to float face up on the water's surface. However, my sister had only finally learned how to swim well enough so that she didn't need

泳ぎながら顔を見合せてにこにこしました。そして波が行ってしまうと三人ながら泳ぎをやめてもとのように底の砂の上に立とうとしました。

ところがどうでしょう、私たちは泳ぎをやめると一しょに、三人ながらずぼりと水の中に潜ってしまいました。水の中に潜っても足は砂にはつかないのです。私たちは驚きました。慌てました。そして一生懸命にめんかきをして、ようやく水の上に顔だけ出すことが出来ました。その時私たち三人が互に見合せた眼といったら、顔といったらありません。顔は真青でした。眼は飛び出しそうに見開いていました。今の波一つでどこか深い所に流されたのだということを私たちはいい合わさないでも知ることが出来たのです。いい合わさないでも私たちは陸の方を眼がけて泳げるだけ泳がなければならないということがわかったのです。

✻✻✻ [PART FOUR] ✻✻✻

三人は黙ったままで体を横にして泳ぎはじめました。けれども私たちにどれほどの力があったかを考えて見て下さい。Mは十四でした。私は十三でした。妹は十一でした。Mは毎年学校の水泳部に行っていたので、とにかくあたり前に泳ぐことを知っていましたが、私は横のし泳ぎを少しと、水の上に仰向けに浮くことを覚えたばかりですし、妹はようやく板を離れて二、三間泳ぐことが出来るだけなのです。

to use a bodyboard, and she was only able to swim about fifteen feet.

We realize also that we were quickly floating out into the open sea. I submerged half of my head while swimming on my side, and sometimes I would try to lift my head. Every time I did this, I saw that my little sister was floating away from me out to the open sea, and my friend M was swimming away from me towards the shore again. After a while, we had drifted so far apart that our voices barely reached each other. Each time a wave came, I would lose sight of either my little sister or M. When my face came into view, my sister called out in a pained voice from behind, "Brother, please come help me ... I'm sinking ... I can't do this!" My sister was sinking; because the water was practically up to her nose when she tried to call out, she seemed to swallow some water and stared at me with a pained expression on her pale face. As I swam ahead, my heart wanted nothing else but to go back for her. I thought about swimming back to where she was many times. But it seems I was a bad person; in situations like that, I just wanted to save my own life. If I went to my little sister, we would both be taken out into the open sea, and I knew that we would both die. That terrified me. In any case, I thought that the only option was to quickly get to the shore and get help from someone, like a fisherman. In retrospect, that seemed like a sneaky thought.

But anyway, as I was thinking that, I concentrated on swimming towards the shore, not looking back. When it started to seem like I was losing my strength, I floated on my back on the water's surface to catch my breath. Even so, the shore seemed like it was getting closer, little by little. I kept swimming as hard as I could; I tried treading water, and then I tried touching my feet to the sand, but they just plunged straight down, and I was submerged up to my head. I was panicking. But I started swimming again, as hard as I could.

御覧なさい私たちは見る見る沖の方へ沖の方へと流されているのです。私は頭を半分水の中につけて横のしでおよぎながら時々頭を上げて見ると、その度ごとに妹は沖の方へと私から離れてゆき、友達のMはまた岸の方へと私から離れて行って、暫らくの後には三人はようやく声がとどく位お互に離ればなれになってしまいました。そして波が来るたんびに私は妹を見失ったりMを見失ったりしました。私の顔が見えると妹は後の方からあらん限りの声をしぼって

「兄さん来てよ……もう沈む……苦しい」

と呼びかけるのです。実際妹は鼻の所位まで水に沈みながら声を出そうとするのですから、その度ごとに水を呑むと見えて真蒼な苦しそうな顔をして私を睨みつけるように見えます。私も前に泳ぎながら心は後にばかり引かれました。幾度も妹のいる方へ泳いで行こうかと思いました。けれども私は悪い人間だったと見えて、こうなると自分の命が助かりたかったのです。妹の所へ行けば、二人とも一緒に沖に流されて命がないのは知れ切っていました。私はそれが恐ろしかったのです。何しろ早く岸について漁夫にでも助けに行ってもらう外はないと思いました。今から思うとそれはずるい考えだったようです。

でもとにかくそう思うと私はもう後も向かずに無我夢中で岸の方を向いて泳ぎ出しました。力が無くなりそうになると仰向に水の上に臥て暫らく気息をつきました。それでも岸は少しずつ近づいて来るようでした。一生懸命に……一生懸命に……、そして立泳ぎのようになって足を砂につけて見ようとしたら、またずぶりと頭まで潜ってしまいました。私は慌てました。そしてまた一生懸命で泳ぎ出しました。

❊❊❊ [PART FIVE] ❊❊❊

It was after a considerable amount of time had passed that I found that I had gotten close enough to the shore that the water only came up to my knees when I tried to stand. I was relieved to be safe, and then I ran around the beach in a daze, crying out like a madman, "Please help!"

When I looked, M was far away on the other side of the beach doing the same thing. Even while I was running around, I didn't forget to look out towards my sister. I could barely see my poor little sister's head, bobbing up and down in the waves, far away from the water's edge.

There were no boats on the seashore, and no fishermen. At that moment, I felt like I wanted to dive into the water again. The thought of abandoning my precious little sister was becoming too unbearable.

Then, M came running from the far side of the beach, pulling a young man by his sleeve. When I saw them, I forgot about everything else and started running towards them. The person I called "young man" must have been a local. He was a passer-by who didn't look like a fisherman, and he was carrying something on his shoulder.

"Quickly ... Please, quickly go save my little sister ... She's over there, over there!" I was crying uncontrollably, pleading so intensely that I was almost stomping my feet. I extended a shaking hand to point toward my little sister's head, barely visible above the water.

The young man looked to where I was pointing and soon put down what he was carrying onto the sand, unwrapped his sash, and put his clothing down together with it. With a splash, he dove into the water.

While I was shaking and crying, I took my fingers from both my hands and jammed them into my mouth, biting down on them hard, as the man who I sent off was steadily going farther out to sea. I didn't know where

＊＊＊ [PART FIVE] ＊＊＊

立って見たら水が膝の所位しかない所まで泳いで来ていたのはそれからよほどたってのことでした。ほっと安心したと思うと、もう夢中で私は泣声を立てながら、

「助けてくれえ」

といって砂浜を気狂いのように駈けずり廻りました。見るとMは遥かむこうの方で私と同じようなことをしています。私は駈けずりまわりながらも妹の方を見ることを忘れはしませんでした。波打際から随分遠い所に、波に隠れたり現われたりして、可哀そうな妹の頭だけが見えていました。

浜には船もいません、漁夫もいません。その時になって私はまた水の中に飛び込んで行きたいような心持ちになりました。大事な妹を置きっぱなしにして来たのがたまらなく悲しくなりました。

その時Mが遥かむこうから一人の若い男の袖を引ぱってこっちに走って来ました。私はそれを見ると何もかも忘れてそっちの方に駈け出しました。若い男というのは、土地の者ではありましょうが、漁夫とも見えないような通りがかりの人で、肩に何か担っていました。

「早く……早く行って助けて下さい……あすこだ、あすこだ」

私は、涙を流し放題に流して、地だんだをふまないばかりにせき立てて、震える手をのばして妹の頭がちょっぴり水の上に浮んでいる方を指しました。

若い男は私の指す方を見定めていましたが、やがて手早く担っていたものを砂の上に卸し、帯をくるくると解いて、衣物を一緒にその上におくと、ざぶりと波を切って海の中にはいって行ってくれました。

my feet were standing, or whether it was cold or hot. I didn't even know whether I had limbs or not.

*** **[PART SIX]** ***

The head of the young man, who was swimming the over-arm stroke, gradually got smaller as he drew closer to my little sister. White foam shined brightly around the man's body, and his hands that cut through the water were sparkling, looking like flying fish that dove up and down. I didn't take my eyes off him.

At last, the young man's head and my little sister's approached each other. I unconsciously took my fingers out of my mouth and went into the water while crying out. But the two of them were coming towards me very, very slowly. For no reason, I leapt onto the sand again, and then I went back into the water. No matter what, I couldn't stand still and wait.

My little sister's head sunk under the water many times. At times, her head was out of sight for so long that I wondered if she had completely sunk. Sometimes, the young man also disappeared from above the surface. But whenever I thought that he was gone, he would suddenly reappear high above the water as he surged forward. It was quite strange looking, so much so that it seemed like they were dancing while swimming. Even so, the two of them were gradually coming closer to the shore, and they finally reached the point where I could even see their faces clearly. However, the waves were beating and crashing against the shore in that area, so there were many times when they were both hidden by whirlpools of white foam. Before long, the young man reached the water's edge, looking like he was crawling. Even though they had reached such a shallow part, my little sister was being carried on the young man's back. I couldn't control my excitement, and ran toward them.

私はぶるぶる震えて泣きながら、両手の指をそろえて口の中へ押こんで、それをぎゅっと歯でかみしめながら、その男がどんどん沖の方に遠ざかって行くのを見送りました。私の足がどんな所に立っているのだか、寒いのだか、暑いのだか、すこしも私には分りません。手足があるのだかないのだかそれも分りませんでした。

✻✻✻ [PART SIX] ✻✻✻

抜手を切って行く若者の頭も段々小さくなりまして、妹との距たりが見る見る近よって行きました。若者の身のまわりには白い泡がきらきらと光って、水を切った手が濡れたまま飛魚が飛ぶように海の上に現われたり隠れたりします。私はそんなことを一生懸命に見つめていました。

とうとう若者の頭と妹の頭とが一つになりました。私は思わず指を口の中から放して、声を立てながら水の中にはいってゆきました。けれども二人がこっちに来るののおそいことおそいこと。私はまた何の訳もなく砂の方に飛び上りました。そしてまた海の中にはいって行きました。如何してもじっとして待っていることが出来ないのです。

妹の頭は幾度も水の中に沈みました。時には沈み切りに沈んだのかと思うほど長く現われて来ませんでした。若者も如何かすると水の上には見えなくなりました。そうかと思うと、ぽこんと跳ね上るように高く水の上に現われ出ました。何んだか曲泳ぎでもしているのではないかと思われるほどでした。それでもそんなことをしている中に、二人は段々岸近くなって来て、とうとうその顔までがはっきり見える位になりました。が、そこいらは打寄せる波が崩れるところなので、

✻✻✻ **[PART SEVEN]** ✻✻✻

As I ran toward them, I was surprised by how the young man looked. He was panting, and his body looked exhausted. When my little sister saw that I was getting closer, she rushed towards me like she was crazy, but she suddenly avoided me and started running toward the sand dunes, as if she had changed her mind. At that moment, I realized that my little sister resented me. When I realized that her reaction was understandable, it made me feel extremely lonely.

Nevertheless, I wondered where my friend M had gone off to, and I scanned my surroundings while standing by the young man's side. He was far away, helping our grandmother while running down a sand dune. I realized that my little sister had already discovered that, and that she was trying to go towards them.

That made me feel a little relieved. I put my hand on the man's shoulder and tried to say something, but he seemed annoyed and brushed off my hand. He sat down where the water was only gently lapping, and with an irritated face he rubbed circles on his chest. I wasn't even sure what I should say to him, so I just stood there in silence, hesitating.

"Good heavens, you saved my granddaughter! I can't thank you enough," I heard my grandmother say earnestly, while panting right beside me. My little sister, soaked from head to toe, was being held by her tightly while sobbing.

The three of us returned to the house with our grandmother, still wet, holding our kimonos and towels under our arms. The young man had finally stood up and dried himself off. He tried to leave, but because my grandmother stood up and insisted, he followed silently behind us.

二人はもろともに幾度も白い泡の渦巻の中に姿を隠しました。やがて若者は這うようにして波打際にたどりつきました。妹はそんな浅みに来ても若者におぶさりかかっていました。私は有頂天になってそこまで飛んで行きました。

✻✻✻ [PART SEVEN] ✻✻✻

飛んで行って見て驚いたのは若者の姿でした。せわしく深く気息をついて、体はつかれ切ったようにゆるんでへたへたになっていました。妹は私が近づいたのを見ると夢中で飛んで来ましたがふっと思いかえしたように私をよけて砂山の方を向いて駈け出しました。その時私は妹が私を恨んでいるのだなと気がついて、それは無理のないことだと思うと、この上なく淋しい気持ちになりました。

それにしても友達のMは何所に行ってしまったのだろうと思って、私は若者のそばに立ちながらあたりを見廻すと、遥かな砂山の所をお婆様を助けながら駈け下りて来るのでした。妹は早くもそれを見付けてそっちに行こうとしているのだとわかりました。

それで私は少し安心して、若者の肩に手をかけて何かいおうとすると、若者はうるさそうに私の手を払いのけて、水の寄せたり引いたりする所に坐りこんだまま、いやな顔をして胸のあたりを撫でまわしています。私は何んだか言葉をかけるのさえためらわれて黙ったまま突立っていました。

「まああなたがこの子を助けて下さいましたんですね。お礼の申しようも御座んせん」

すぐそばで気息せき切ってしみじみといわれるお婆様の声を私は聞きました。妹は頭からずぶ濡れになったままで泣

✻✻✻ **[PART EIGHT]** ✻✻✻

When we arrived at the house, a bed for my little sister had already been prepared. She changed into her pajamas, and once she was put to bed, she looked as if she were dreaming; her temperature went up and she started shaking like a leaf. Our grandmother was a stout-hearted person. Once she had finished diligently taking care of my little sister, she turned to the young man and thanked him from the bottom of her heart. The young man was the type of person who did not even utter a greeting, and he only nodded his head silently. My grandmother managed to get him to tell her where he lived. While he was drinking barley tea, the young man turned toward my little sister with a worried expression on his face, bowed a few times, and left for home.

"When M ran here and told me what had happened, I felt like I was going to faint. Your father and mother trusted me to take care of you, and if something had happened, if you had died, I wouldn't have been able to live. So I was prepared to die, and I ran up the sand dune faster than M. Even though that man just happened to be there to help, it was still terrifying. If you don't start being more careful from now on, we're really going to be in trouble."

My grandmother said this sternly, looking at me while I was seated in front of her. She was normally very nice, but at that time, her words made my body and my heart freeze with fear. Even though it was for a very short time, I did think about saving only myself. Knowing that, it felt like my mind was being poked with needles all over. I couldn't cry even if I wanted to, and I tensed up and continued to sit in front of my grandmother, looking down. The heat of the unyielding sun blazed down on the sand surrounding the wooden hallway outside the sliding doors.

きじゃくりをしながらお婆様にぴったり抱かれていました。
　私たち三人は濡れたままで、衣物やタオルを小脇に抱えてお婆様と一緒に家の方に帰りました。若者はようやく立上って体を拭いて行ってしまおうとするのをお婆様がたって頼んだので、黙ったまま私たちのあとから跟いて来ました。

＊＊＊ [PART EIGHT] ＊＊＊

家に着くともう妹のために床がとってありました。妹は寝衣に着かえて臥かしつけられると、まるで夢中になってしまって、熱を出して木の葉のようにふるえ始めました。お婆様は気丈な方で甲斐々々しく世話をすますと、若者に向って心の底からお礼をいわれました。若者は挨拶の言葉も得いわないような人で、唯黙ってうなずいてばかりいました。お婆様はようやくのことでその人の住っている所だけを聞き出すことが出来ました。若者は麦湯を飲みながら、妹の方を心配そうに見てお辞儀を二、三度して帰って行ってしまいました。
「Mさんが駈けこんで来なすって、お前たちのことをいいなすった時には、私は眼がくらむようだったよ。おとうさんやお母さんから頼まれていて、お前たちが死にでもしたら、私は生きてはいられないから一緒に死ぬつもりであの砂山をお前、Mさんより早く駈け上りました。でもあの人が通り合せたお蔭で助かりはしたもののこわいことだったねえ、もうもう気をつけておくれでないとほんに困りますよ」
　お婆様はやがてきっとなって私を前にすえてこう仰有いました。日頃はやさしいお婆様でしたが、その時の言葉には私は身も心もすくんでしまいました。少しの間でも自分一人が助かりたいと思った私は、心の中をそこら中から針でつか

My grandmother went herself to the young man's home to thank him. She brought something for him as a sign of her heartfelt appreciation, but it seemed that the young man wouldn't take it no matter what she said.

For five or six years after that, we knew the young man's whereabouts. But now, we don't know where he is or how he is doing. Our lovely grandmother has departed from this world. My friend M was murdered in mysterious circumstances. Now, only my younger sister and I survive. Every time I talk about that day to my sister, she always says that at that time, she really resented me. When I think about how, at that time, my little sister would disappear whenever a wave rose, my heart beats fast in my chest even now, and a vague feeling of dread washes over me.

れるようでした。私は泣くにも泣かれないでかたくなったままこちんとお婆様の前に下を向いて坐りつづけていました。しんしんと暑い日が縁の向うの砂に照りつけていました。

若者の所へはお婆様が自分で御礼に行かれました。そして何か御礼の心でお婆様が持って行かれたものをその人は何んといっても受取らなかったそうです。

それから五、六年の間はその若者のいる所は知れていましたが、今は何処にどうしているのかわかりません。私たちのいいお婆様はもうこの世にはおいでになりません。私の友達のMは妙なことから人に殺されて死んでしまいました。妹と私ばかりが今でも生き残っています。その時の話を妹にするたんびに、あの時ばかりは兄さんを心から恨めしく思ったと妹はいつでもいいます。波が高まると妹の姿が見えなくなったその時の事を思うと、今でも私の胸は動悸がして、空恐ろしい気持ちになります。

⁂ [LESSON FOR PART ONE] ⁂

Translator's Notes

1. 土用波 **doyōnami** is a culture-specific notion. 土用 **doyō** refers to the transition period between seasons based on Wu Xing (五行 **gogyō**), an ancient Chinese philosophy. **Doyōnami** 土用波 is the starting point of the story, so instead of replacing it with a notion close to that in the West, 土用 was directly rendered as "*doyo*" while 波 **nami** was rendered as "wave," to show the readers that 土用波 **doyōnami** is a kind of wave.
2. There is no perfect English equivalent for お名残だといって **onagori da to itte**, so it was explained in the translation.
3. There is no explicit linguistic clue that shows the gender of M in the Japanese text. However, we assumed that M is a male and used the male version of the English third person pronoun.

Vocabulary and Expressions

- 溺(おぼ)れる **oboreru** to drown
- …かける **... kakeru** to be about to ...

  EXAMPLE:

  溺(おぼ)れかけました。

  Oborekake mashita.

  (I) was about to drown.
- 土用波(どようなみ) **doyōnami** high waves during the late summer.
- 波(なみ) **nami** wave
- 風(かぜ) **kaze** wind
- …のに **... no ni** although ...

  EXAMPLE:

  まだ夏(なつ)なのにすずしいです。

  Mada natsu na no ni suzushii desu.

  It's cool although it's still summer.
- 海岸(かいがん) **kaigan** coast
- 打(う)ち寄(よ)せる **uchi-yoseru** to break onto (shore)
- …頃(ころ) **... koro** around the time when ...
- …と… **... to ...** [GRAMMAR] when/once ..., then ...; と **to** follows a verb or an adjective in the

present plain form, and connects two clauses that express an automatic or generic consequence if the main sentence is in the present tense.

EXAMPLE:

おすと、あきます。

Osu to, akimasu.

Once you push it, it opens.

- 海水浴 **kaisuiyoku** swimming in the ocean
- 都 **miyako** capital city, metropolis
- 段々 **dandan** gradually
- 別荘 **bessō** villa
- しめる = 閉める **shimeru** to close
- …ようになる **... yō ni naru** to start ... [GRAMMAR] You can express a change of state using ようになる.

EXAMPLE:

田中さんは最近よくしゃべるようになりました。

Tanaka-san wa saikin yoku shaberu yō ni narimashita.

Mr. Tanaka started to talk more these days.

- ゆく **yuku** = いく **iku**
- 集まる **atsumaru** to gather (an intransitive counterpart of 集める **atsumeru**)
- …でも **demo** such a thing like ...

EXAMPLE:

コーヒーでもどうですか。

Kōhī demo dō desu ka.

How about a cup of coffee?

- 大勢な **ōzei na** = 大勢の **ōzeio** many (for people)
- 一たい = 一体 **ittai** an intensifier for a content question

EXAMPLE:

一体何がおきたんですか。

Ittai nani ga okitan desu ka.

What happened?

- 見わたす **miwatasu** to look out over
- …かぎり **... kagiri** as far as ...

EXAMPLE:

見わたすかぎり山でした。

Miwatasu-kagiri yama deshita.

There were mountains everywhere as far as I could see.

- 砂 **suna** sand
- 砂山 **sunayama** sand hill, sand dune

- 砂浜(すなはま) **sunahama** sandy beach
- 不思議(ふしぎ) **fushigi** mystery
- 人(ひと)っ子(こ)一人(ひとり)いない **hitokko-hitori inai** There is not a single person.
- 名残(なごり) **nagori** lingering feeling anticipating parting

  EXAMPLE:

  名残(なごり)おしい **nagorioshii** *to feel sorry to part*
- …ことにする **... koto ni suru** to decide on ... [GRAMMAR] You can express your decision by using ことにする.

  EXAMPLE:

  イギリスに行(い)くことにしました。

  Igirisu ni iku koto ni shimashita.

  I decided to go to England.
- 荒(あら)い **arai** rough
- 風(かぜ) **kaze** wind
- なしする **nashi suru** probably it means ない **nai**
- 仰有(おっしゃ)る = 仰(おっしゃ)る **ossharu** to say (honorific)
- 聞(き)かずに **kikazu ni** = 聞(き)かないで **kikanai de**
- 出(で)かける **dekakeru** to go out
- 上天気(じょうてんき) **jō-tenki** fair weather
- 虫(むし)の音(ね) **mushi-no-ne** calls and sounds made by insects
- 裸足(はだし) **hadashi** barefoot
- 駆(か)ける **kakeru** to run
- …ほど **... hodo** to the extent that ...
- 飛(と)ぶ **tobu** to jump, to fly
- 麦稈帽子(むぎわらぼうし) **mugiwara-bōshi** straw hat
- つかる **tsukaru** to be soaked (an intransitive counterpart of つける **tsukeru** to soak)
- …ので **no de** because ... [GRAMMAR] ので follows a clause in the plain form and creates an adverbial clause that expresses the reason or the cause of what is expressed in the main clause.

  EXAMPLE:

  明日(あした)はテストがあるので今日(きょう)は勉強(べんきょう)します。

  Ashita wa tesuto ga aru no de, kyō wa benkyō shimasu.

  I have a test tomorrow, so I will study today.

  The plain non-past affirmative copula だ **da** must be replaced by な **na** when it precedes ので **no de.**

EXAMPLE:
もう秋なので涼しいです。
Mō aki na no de suzushii desu.
Because it is already autumn, it's cool.

- 気息を切る = 息を切る **iki o kiru** to be out of breath
- 急ぐ **isogu** to hurry

Exercises

Select the most appropriate item in the parentheses.

1. 土用波のころになると、風がぜんぜんない（ので・のに）高い波が来ます。

2. 九月になると、海水浴に来ていた人もだんだん帰るよう（で・に）なります。

3. 砂山から見て（いた・いる）と、あんなにたくさんの人はどこから来たのだろうと思えるほどでした。

4. 夏もおわりなので、私と、妹と、友達のMはもう一度泳ぐ（よう・こと）にしました。

5. お婆様がやめた方がいいといいましたが、それを（聞かないで・聞いて）海に行きました。

6. 少しでも早く海につかりたかった（ので・のに）海に向かって走りました。

7. 草の中には（もう・まだ）虫の音がしていました。

8. でも、砂(すな)は熱(あつ)くて裸足(はだし)では砂の上(うえ)をあるけない（より・ほど）でした。

Discussion Questions

1. Find some background information about Arishima Takeo and discuss it.
2. Do research on *doyo* waves and share your findings.
3. Why did the protagonist's grandmother discourage them from swimming on that day? Why did they persist in doing so?

＊＊＊ [LESSON FOR PART TWO] ＊＊＊

Translator's Notes

水を呑ませられる **mizu o nomaserareru** literally means "to be made to swallow water." However, such an expression in English requires an agent for the action although the Japanese expression does not. Hence the causative passive tense is not used in the English sentence.

Vocabulary and Expressions

- 紆波(うねり) **uneri** wave motion, swell
- うつ（打(う)つ） **utsu** to hit
- ちゃぷり **chapuri** [MIMETIC] a small splash
- 波打際(なみうちぎわ)＝波(なみ)打(う)ち際(ぎわ) **namiuchi-giwa** water's edge along the shore
- くだける（砕(くだ)ける） **kudakeru** to break into pieces
- 沖(おき) **oki** open sea, offshore
- 細長(ほそなが)い **hosonagai** long and narrow
- 小山(こやま) **koyama** hill (*lit., small mountain*)
- 陸(りく) **riku** land, shore
- 向(む)く **muku** to face
- 段々(だんだん) **dandan** gradually, increasingly

- 押寄せる **oshi-yoseru** to advance on, to close in, to surge towards
- てっぺん **teppen** top, peak
- 尖る **togaru** to taper to a point
- ざぶり **zaburi** [MIMETIC] a big splash
- 崩れる **kuzureru** to collapse
- …かかる **... kakaru** to be on the verge of ...

  EXAMPLE:

  崩れかかった **kuzure-kakatta**

  It appeared to start collapsing.
- 暫く **shibaraku** for a while
- 間をおく **ma o oku** to have a short intermission
- 勢い **ikioi** force, vigor
- 這い上がる **haiagaru** to creep up
- そこら中 **sokora-jū** everywhere
- 泡 **awa** bubble, foam
- 敷きつめる **shikitsumeru** to completely cover a surface; to spread all over
- …ような **... yō na** like ... [GRAMMAR] ような creates a **na**-type adjective that expresses a simile. It can follow a noun with the particle の **no**.

  EXAMPLE:

  天使のような人です。

  Tenshi no yō na hito desu.

  She is a person who is just like an angel.

  It can also follow a verb in the plain form.

  EXAMPLE:

  絵に描いたような餅ですね。

  E ni kaita yō na mochi desu ne.

  It is a rice cake that looks like a drawing.
- 様子 **yōsu** appearance
- 気味悪い **kimi-warui** creepy, spooky
- 折角 **sekkaku** with trouble
- …ながら **... nagara** in spite of ..., while ... [GRAMMAR] ながら can follow a verb in the stem form and expresses an accompanying activity. It is often followed by も.

  EXAMPLE:

  文句を言いながらも助けてくれた。

  Monku o iinagara mo tasukete-kureta.

  He helped me in spite of his complaints.

■ そのまま **sono-mama** without change, as it is
■ 引返す **hikikaesu** to go back
■ で **de** = それで **sorede** as a result, therefore
■ 脱がせる **nugaseru** to make someone take off ...
■ 仰向けに **aomuke** facing up
■ 丸めこむ **marumekomu** to roll up
■ 手をつなぐ **te o tsunagu** to hold hands
■ しどいね **shidoi ne** = ひどいね **hidoi ne** (It's) terrible, isn't it?
■ 退く = 引く **hiku** to move back, to recede
■ 力 **chikara** force, power, strength
■ 踝 **kurubushi** ankle
■ 急な **kyū na** rapid, abrupt
■ 河 **kawa** river
■ 流れ **nagare** flow
■ 掘れる **horeru** to dig (intransitive verb)
■ うっかりしていると **ukkari shite-iru to** if one is not alert
■ 倒れる **taoreru** to fall
■ …そうになる **... sō ni naru** to be about to ... [GRAMMAR] そう **sō** follows a verb or an adjective in the stem form and creates a new **na**-type adjective that means "to be about to ..." or "to look like ..."

EXAMPLES:

ころびそうになった。

Korobisō ni natta.

I was about to fall down.

あのバッグは高そうだった。

Ano baggu wa takasō datta.

That bag looked expensive.

■ 位 **kurai** degree, extent
■ 動く **ugoku** to move
■ ふらふら **furafura** [MIMETIC] in an unsteady or unstable state
■ (…て)ならない **(... te-) naranai** to be irresistibly ...

EXAMPLE:

面白くてならない **Omoshiro-kute-naranai** *irresistibly amusing*

■ 足の裏 **ashi no ura** bottom of one's feet
■ くすむる **kusumuru** = くすぐる **kusuguru** to tickle
■ 埋まる **uzumaru** = 埋まる **umaru** to be buried

■ この上なく **kono-ue naku** extremely

■ …まま **... mama** while keeping ... [GRAMMAR] まま follows a verb in the plain past form, an adjective in the pre-nominal form, a noun followed by の **no** or a demonstrative adjective, and expresses a situation where the same state is maintained.

EXAMPLES:

ドアを開けたまま出かけました。

Doa o aketamama dekakemashita.

(He) went out, leaving the door open.

靴のままうちにはいりました。

Kutsu no mama uchi ni hairimashita.

I entered my house with my shoes on.

■ 深い **fukai** deep

■ 膝 **hiza** knee

■ くの字に曲る **ku-no-ji ni magaru** to be bent to form the shape of the hiragana character く.

■ 向脛 **mukōzune** shin

■ あたる(当たる) **ataru** to hit

■ 痛い **itai** painful

■ 揃える **soroeru** to put ... together and in order

■ 勝 **kachi** nominal form of the verb 勝つ **katsu** to win

■ 片足で立ちっこ **kata'ashi de tachikko** the game of standing on one leg

■ 人魚 **ningyo** mermaid

■ 跳ね廻る **hane-mawaru** to jump around

■ …度ごとに **... tabi goto ni** every time ...

■ 背伸び **senobi** standing on tiptoes

■ 深味 **fukami** deeper area

■ 進む **susumu** to go forward

■ 腰 **koshi** waist

■ 追付く(おっつく **ottsuku** = おいつく **oitsuku**) to catch up

■ ふわり **fuwari** [MIMETIC] soft, gentle, or light state

■ 浮き上る **uki-agaru** to float up

■ 水を呑ませられる **mizu o nomaserareru** to be made to swallow water

Exercises

Select the most appropriate item in the parentheses.

1. うねりとは（小さい・大きい）波です。

2. 沖の方に細長い小山（な・の）ような波ができて、それが陸の方に押寄せて来ます。

3. それから、その小山のてっぺんが尖って、（ざぶり・ちゃぷり）と大きい音をたてて崩れます。

4. そうすると、ひどい勢いで砂の上に這い上がってきて、砂浜はすべて真っ白な泡（を・で）いっぱいになります。

5. 三人はうねりを見て気味悪く思いましたが、（せっかく・早く）ここまで来て帰るのはいやでした。

6. それで、三人は手をつないで水の中（に・で）入って行きました。

7. Mが『ひき』が（ある・ひどい）と言いました。

8. でも、いっしょに波で（あそび・あそぶ）ながら、だんだん深みに進みました。

9. 波が来ると（立った・立つ）ままではいられなくて、ふわっと浮かなくてはならないほどでした。

Discussion Questions

1. How is the **hiki** pull described in this story?

2. What kind of games did they play in the ocean? Have you played similar games?

⁂ [LESSON FOR PART THREE] ⁂

Translator's Notes

The use of color terms varies across cultures. The color "blue" is used not only for the "blue" in blue sky, but also the "green" of leafy vegetables, and even for the paleness of a person's face. To render 顔(かお)は真青(まっさお)でした **kao wa massao deshita** while maintaining a sense of "blue," we added "lips" as in, "Our faces and lips were a bluish pale."

Vocabulary and Expressions

- 地面(じめん) **jimen** ground (sea floor in this case)
- (…て) も **(... te) mo** even though ..., even if ... [GRAMMAR] By adding the particle も after a verb in the **te**-form, you can create a concessive clause that means "even if ..." or "even though."

  EXAMPLE:

  三回(さんかい)読(よ)んでもわかりませんでした。

  San-kai yonde mo wakarimasen deshita.

  I couldn't understand (it) even though I read (it) three times.
- 背中(せなか) **senaka** back (of a body)
- ざぶん **zabun** [MIMETIC] big splash
- 一面(いちめん)に **ichimen ni** all over the surface
- いきなり **ikinari** suddenly
- 手(て)に取(と)るように **te ni toru yō ni** clearly, quite distinctly (*lit., just like we can touch it by hand*)

EXAMPLE:
あなたの気持ちは手に取るように分かります。
Anata no kimochi wa te ni toru yō ni wakarimasu.
I understood your feeling very clearly.

- この上なく **kono-ue naku** more than anything else
- あぶない（危ない） **abunai** dangerous
- 忘れる **wasureru** to forget
- 波越 **funakoshi** wave-passing
- 遊び **asobi** play, game
- 続けさまに **tsuzuke-sama ni** continuously
- あら **ara** Oh! (an interjection used by female)
- 来てよ **kite yo** = 来たわよ **kitawa yo** female version of 来たよ **kita yo** Here it comes!
- いきなり **ikinari** suddenly
- 思わず **omowazu** reflexively
- …の言葉通りに **... no kotoba dōri ni** exactly as ... said
- かけはなれて **kakehanarete** be far apart from the rest
- ひろげる **hirogeru** to spread, extend
- 恰好 = 格好 **kakkō** shape, form, figure, posture
- 気味悪そうに **kimi-warusō ni** feeling spooky/creepy
- いくらかでも **ikuraka demo** even a little bit, any amount/distance
- 浅い **asai** shallow
- 遁げる = 逃げる **nigeru** to run away
- いうまでもない **iu made mo nai** needless to say
- のめる **nomeru** to fall forward
- 突出す **tsukidashu** to stick out
- ひどい **hidoi** terrible
- 思うように **omou yō ni** as we intend
- 奴 **yatsu** a person (derogatory term)
- 追いかける **oikakeru** to chase
- 見る見る **mirumiru** before our eyes
- ちらり **chirari** [MIMETIC] glancing
- …始める **... hajimeru** to start ...

[GRAMMAR] 始める can follow a verb in the stem form to mean "to start -ing."

EXAMPLE:

昨日この本を読み始めました。

Kinō kono hon o yomihajime mashita.

I started to read this book.

- 大声 **ōgoe** loud voice
- 巻き込む **maki-komu** to involve, to drag into
- 越す **kosu** to go across, to go over
- そういわれればそうです **sō iwarereba sō desu** That seems to be right.
- 立止まる **tachidomaru** to stop and stand still
- 屏風 **byōbu** folding screen
- 立てつらねる **tatetsuraneru** to build ... and line them up
- もむ（揉む） **momu** to massage, to rub
- 感じる **kanjiru** to feel, to sense
- やりすごす **yarisugosu** to let something go past
- ようやく **yōyaku** finally, barely
- 安心する **anshin suru** to feel safe
- 顔を見合せる **kao o miawaseru** to exchange glances, to look at each other's face
- もとのように **moto no yō ni** like before
- 底 **soko** bottom
- 立とうとする **tatō to suru** to try to stand
- …とする **... to suru** to try to ... [GRAMMAR] とする follows a verb in the volitional form and expresses one's attempt, which is usually not realized.

EXAMPLE:

うそをつこうとしましたがつけませんでした。

Uso o tsukō to shimashita ga tsukemasen deshita.

I tried to lie, but I couldn't.

- ところがどうでしょう **tokoro ga dō deshō** on the contrary (*lit., however, do you know what is the case?*)
- ずぼりと **zobori to** [MIMETIC] vigorously

- 潜る **kuguru** to go under
- 驚く **odoroku** to be shocked
- 慌てる **awateru** to panic
- めんかき **menkaki** a type of swimming stroke, probably similar to doggy paddle
- …たらない **-tara nai** there is nothing like ...
- 真青 **massao** very pale
- 見開く **mihiraku** to widely open (one's eyes)
- 流す **nagasu** to wash away
- 眼がける = 目がける **megakeru** to aim at
- …なければならない **... nakereba naranai** must do ..., to have to do ... [GRAMMAR] A verb in the negative **ba**-conditional form can be used along with ならない **naranai** or いけない **ikenai** to express an obligation.

EXAMPLE:

明日6時に起きなければなりません。

Ashita roku-ji ni okinakereaba narimasen.

I have to wake up at 6 a.m. tomorrow.

Exercises

Select the most appropriate item in the parentheses.

1. 波が来てふわりと浮き上がると、（高い・ひくい）ところに来たように思いました。

2. 波が行って地面に足を（ついた・つく）と、波の背で岸がみえませんでした。

3. しばらく波こしの遊びをしていると、後ろ（から・まで）大きな波が来ました。

4. 波がくだけるところに（行く・行かない）と巻き込まれるとMが言いました

5. それで、その場（で・に）波をやりすごしました。

6. しかし、足を（つく・つこう）とすると、潜ってしまいました。

7. いくら足をつこうと（して・する）も、足は海の底の砂につきませんでした。

8. ひきがつよくて、三人はずっと（沖・浅い所）に連れて行かれたのでした。

9. 一生懸命、めんかきをして、（顔・足・手）を出しました。

10. 何も言わなくても岸に向かって泳げるだけ泳がなければ（ならない・なる）と分かりました。

Discussion Questions

1. Do you think M's warning was helpful? Why?

2. If you suddenly realized that your feet could not reach the floor of the ocean, what would you do?

✻✻✻ [LESSON FOR PART FOUR] ✻✻✻

Translator's Notes

Measurement units are culture-specific, and in some cases, the quantity or amount must be accurately converted using the units used in the culture of the target language. However, in other cases, simplified numbers can be used depending on the context. Since the little sister's approximate swimming ability in this section of the story is quite important, the length expressed by 間 **ken** is converted to approximate length expressed by foot.

Vocabulary and Expressions

- 体 **karada** body
- 水泳部 **suieibu** swimming club
- あたり前に **atarimae ni** obviously
- 横のし泳ぎ **yokonoshi-oyogi** sidestroke (swimming)
- 浮く **uku** to float
- 覚えたばかりだ **oboetabakari da** to have just learned
- ようやく **yōyaku** barely
- 板 **ita** board
- 離れる **hanareru** to leave, to go away, to be separated
- …間 **...** old measurement unit in Japan, approximately 6 feet
- 流される **nagasareru** to be washed away (the causative form of 流す **nagasu**)
- その度ごとに **sono tabi goto ni** every occasion of it, every time
- 岸 **kishi** coast, shore
- とどく（届く）**todoku** to reach
- 離ればなれになる **hanare-banare ni naru** to be separated
- …たんびに **... tanbi ni** = …度に **... tabi ni** every time ...

EXAMPLE:

あの店に行くたんびに一万円使ってしまいます。

Ano mise ni iku tanbi ni ichi-man-en tsukatte shimaimasu.

Every time I go there, I end up spending 10,000 yen.

- 見失う **miushinau** to lose sight of
- あらん限り **aran-kagiri** as much as possible
- しぼる **shiboru** to squeeze
- 沈む **shizumu** to sink
- 苦しい **kurushii** to be distressed, discomforted, painful
- 実際 **jissai** in reality
- 睨みつける **nirami-tsukeru** to stare at
- 幾度も **ikudo mo** = 何度も **nando mo** numerous times
- 命 **inochi** life
- 恐ろしい **osoroshii** fearful
- 漁夫 = 漁師 **ryōshi** fishermen
- ... する外はない **... suru hoka wa nai** there is no solution other than ...

- 今から思うと **ima kara omou to** as I think about it now, in retrospect
- ずるい **zurui** sly, sneaky
- 後ろも向かずに **ushiro mo mukazu ni** without facing back
- 無我夢中で **muga-muchū de** being absorbed in, losing oneself in
- …出す **... dasu** to abruptly start doing ... [GRAMMAR] 出す follows a verb in the stem form and means "to abruptly start doing."

  EXAMPLE:

  妹は泣き出しました。

  Imōto wa nakidashi mashita.

  My little sister burst into tears.
- 仰向け **aomuke** facing up
- 気息＝息 **iki** breath
- 気息をつく＝息をつく **iki o tsuku** to breathe
- 近づく **chikazuku** to become closer, to approach
- 一生懸命に **isshō-kenmei ni** with all one's might
- 立ち泳ぎ **tachi-oyogi** treading water
- ずぶり **zuburi** [MIMETIC] abrupt plunge

Exercises

Select the most appropriate item in the parentheses.

1. 三人は（黙る・黙った）まま泳ぎはじめました。

2. 妹はだんだん（沖・岸）の方へと離れていきました。

3. Mはだんだん（沖・岸）の方へと離れていきました。

4. 私の顔が（見る・見える）と、妹は「兄さん来てよ。」と呼びかけました。

5. 妹は鼻のところまで（沈み・沈んで）ながら声を出そうとしていました。

6. それで、水を（飲んで・飲む・飲み）しまったと思います。

7. 幾度も妹の方へ泳いで行こうか（と・に）思いました。

8. でも、早く岸について漁師にでも（助ける・助けて）もらうしかないと思いました。

9. いっしょうけんめい泳いで、（疲れる・疲れた）と仰向けにねて息をしました。

Discussion Questions

1. Compare your swimming skills with that of the characters in this story.
2. Describe the emotions of the protagonist, being placed between M and his sister right in the ocean.
3. What kind of person did the protagonist think he was on this day?

✻✻✻ [LESSON FOR PART FIVE] ✻✻✻

Translator's Notes

The Japanese clausal connective particle が **ga** does not always represent conflict or contrast. It may simply connect clauses to show a transition, and can be translated as either "but" or "and." For example, translating が **ga** in 若い男は私の指す方を見定めていましたが、やがて… **wakai otoko wa watashi no sasu hō o misadamete-imashita ga, yagate ...** as "but" does not make sense, and it can be translated as "and."

Vocabulary and Expressions

- よほど **yohodo** to a large extent
- 安心する **anshin suru** to be relieved
- 夢中で **muchū de** in a daze
- 気狂い = 気違い **kichigai** crazy
- 駈けずり廻る = 駈けずり回る **kakezuri mawaru** to run around
- 随分 **zuibun** quite
- 隠れる **kakureru** to hide
- 現れる **arawareru** to appear
- 浜 **hama** beach, seashore
- 心持ち **kokoro-mochi** feeling, mood
- 置きっぱなし **okippanashi** to leave something/someone behind
- たまらなく **tamaranaku** unbearably
- 遥かむこうから **haruka mukō kara** from far away
- 袖 **sode** sleeve
- 土地の者 **tochi no mono** local person
- 通りがかりの人 **tōrigakari no hito** passer-by
- 担う **ninau** to carry
- あすこだ **asuko da** = あそこだ **asoko da**
- …放題 **... hōdai** as much as one would like to ...

  EXAMPLE:

  食べ放題です。

  Tabehōdai desu.

  You can eat as much as you want. (buffet style)
- 地だんだをふむ **jidanda o fumu** to stamp one's feet (in frustration, impatience, etc.)
- せき立てる **seki-tateru** to urge on
- 震える **furueru** to tremble, to shiver
- のばす **nobasu** to extend
- 指す **sasu** to point at
- 見定める **misadameru** to confirm
- 手早く **tebayaku** quickly
- 卸す = 下す **orosu** to put down
- 帯 **obi** *obi*, kimono sash
- 解く **toku** to untie, to unwrap
- 衣物 = 着物 **kimono** clothing
- 切る **kiru** to cut
- 波を切る **nami o kiru** to cut one's way through the waves
- ぶるぶる **buruburu** [MIMETIC] shivering

■ 指 **yubi** fingers
■ 押こむ = 押し込む **oshikomu** to push ... into ...
■ ぎゅっと **gyutto** [MIMETIC] tightly, firmly
■ かみしめる **kamishimeru** to bite firmly
■ 遠ざかる **tōzakaru** to go away
■ 見送る **miokuru** to see someone off

Exercises

Select the most appropriate item in the parentheses.

1. 立ってみたら水は膝の所くらいまでで、私はやっと安心（する・した・して）と、助けをもとめて駈けずりまわりました。

2. Mも私（と・に）同じようなことをしていました。

3. 浜には船も人もないのを（みる・みた）と、もう一度海へもどって妹のところまで泳ぎたくなりました。

4. 大事な妹をおきっぱなしにしてきたのがたまらなく（悲しく・さみしく）思いました。

5. Mが若い男の人をつれてきました。その人は漁師には（見えました・見えませんでした）。

6. 私は「早く行って（助けて・手伝って）ください。」と男の人に言いました。

7. そして、（ざぶり・ぶるぶる）とふるえながら、妹の方を指しました。

8. 男の人は着ているものをぬいで、（ざぶり・ぶるぶる）と波を切って泳いでいってくれました。

Discussion Questions

1. How do you think the protagonist felt when he saw no one on the shore?

2. How do you think the protagonist felt when M brought a young man?

3. How do you think the protagonist felt when the young man started to swim toward his little sister?

✻✻✻ [LESSON FOR PART SIX] ✻✻✻

Translator's Notes

The description of the protagonist's sister and the young man's struggle in the ocean is mainly described through the position and the movement of their heads as objects rather than people. The perspective was changed in some cases because a direct rendering of such descriptions in English does not always sound natural.

Vocabulary and Expressions

- ■ 抜手 **nukite** over-arm stroke
- ■ 若者 **wakamono** young man
- ■ 距たり = 隔たり **hedatari** distance
- ■ 近寄る **chikayoru** to approach, to come closer
- ■ きらきら **kirakira** [MIMETIC] shining
- ■ 水を切る **mizu o kiru** to cut through the water
- ■ 濡れる **nureru** to get wet
- ■ 飛魚 **tobiuo** flying fish
- ■ 飛ぶ **tobu** to fly
- ■ とうとう **tōtō** finally
- ■ 放す **hanasu** to let something or someone go

■ 何の訳もなく **nan no wake mo naku** without any particular reason

■ 如何しても = どうしても **dōshite mo** no matter what

■ じっと **jitto** [MIMETIC] motionlessly

■ 待つ **matsu** to wait

■ 幾度も **ikudo mo** many times

■ …切る **kiru** to completely ... [GRAMMAR] 切る follows a verb in the stem form and shows that the action is performed completely.

EXAMPLE:

紙を使い切ってしまった。

Kami o tsukaikitte-shimatta.

I used up the paper.

■ ぽこん **pokon** [MIMETIC] a plop

■ 曲泳ぎ **kyoku-oyogi** swimming to the music

■ が **ga** = ですが , ところが **desu ga, tokoro ga**

■ そこいら **sokoira** around that area

■ 渦巻き **uzumaki** whirlpool

■ 姿 **sugata** figure, appearance

■ 浅み **asami** shallow area

■ おぶさる **obusaru** to be carried on someone else's back (an intransitive counterpart of おぶる **oburu**)

■ 有頂天 **uchōten** ecstasy

Exercises

Select the most appropriate item in the parentheses.

1. 若者の頭はだんだん（小さい・小さく）なりました。

2. だんだん妹に（近く・遠く）なって行きました。

3. 若者のまわりには白い泡が（ひらひら・きらきら）光っていました。

4. とうとう若者の頭と妹の頭が一つ（に・が）なりました。

5. 若者と妹は見えなく（したり・なったり）、水の上に現れたりしました。

6. でも、二人はだんだん（岸・沖）に近くなって来ました。

7. 若者は（飛ぶ・這う）ようにして波打際につきました。

8. 妹は浅いところに来ても若者（で・に）おぶさりかかっていました。

9. 私は（有頂天・渦巻き）になってそこまで飛んでいきました。

Discussion Questions

1. How do you think the young man's swimming appeared to the protagonist?

2. What sort of different metaphors can you think of for describing the young man's swimming?

＊＊＊ [LESSON FOR PART SEVEN] ＊＊＊

Vocabulary and Expressions

- せわしい **sewashii** hectic
- ゆるむ **yurumu** to relax
- へたへた **hetaheta** [MIMETIC] collapsing, lacking the energy to stand
- 思いかえす **omoi-kaesu** to reconsider
- よける **yokeru** to avert, to avoid
- 恨む **uramu** to bear a grudge, to resent
- 気がつく **ki ga tsuku** to notice
- 無理のないこと **muri no nai koto** not unreasonable
- 淋しい **sabishii** lonely

- 見廻す **mimawasu** to look around
- 肩 **kata** shoulder
- うるさそうに **urusasō ni** appearing to be annoyed
- 払いのける **harai-nokeru** to brush away
- 坐る＝座る **suwaru** to sit
- 胸 **mune** chest
- 撫でる **naderu** to rub
- ためらう **tamerau** to hesitate
- 突立つ **tsuttatsu** to stand in one place doing nothing in particular
- まあ **mā** Oh dear! (used in female speech)
- お礼の申しようも御座んせん **orei no mōshiyō mo gozansen** I don't know how to thank you.
- しみじみと **shimijimi to** heartily
- ずぶ濡れ **zubunure** soaked
- 泣きじゃくる **nakijakuru** to sob
- ぴったり **pittari** [MIMETIC] tightly
- 抱く **daku** to embrace
- 小脇に抱え **kowaki ni kakae** to hold something under one's arm
- 拭く **fuku** to wipe
- 頼む **tanomu** to request
- 黙る **damaru** to be silent
- 跟いて来る＝ついて来る **tsuite-kuru** to follow (me/us)

Exercises

Select the most appropriate item in the parentheses.

1. 若者はびっくりするほどせわしく深く息をついて、疲れ切って（へたへた・かたかた）になっていました。

2. 妹は私を（見る・見た）と、私の方に駆けて来ました。

3. しかし、ふっと思い返したように、急に（私・波）をよけて砂山の方に走り出しました。

4. 私は妹は私を（恨んで・まって）いるのだと思い、淋しい気持ちになりました。

5. 若者のそばに（すわり・立ち）ながらあたりを見まわすと、Mとおばあさんが砂山を駆け下りて来るのが見えました。

6. 妹はおばあさんの方に（向かった・向かって）駆けて行きました。

7. 若者はいやな顔をしてだまった（まま・つづけて）すわって胸を撫でていました。

8. おばあさんは若者にお礼の申し（よう・方）もないほどありがたく思っているといいました。

9. 皆、家の方にあるきはじめ、若者はおばあさんが頼んだ（ので・のに）いっしょについて行きました。

Discussion Questions

1. Why do you think the protagonist felt a little better when he realized that his sister was running toward their grandmother?

2. How do you think the protagonist felt when he was standing next to the young man? Why?

✻✻✻ [LESSON FOR PART EIGHT] ✻✻✻

Vocabulary and Expressions

- 着く **tsuku** to arrive
- 床をとる **toko o toru** to lay out the futon (Japanese bedding)
- (…て) ある **(...te) aru** to have been done [GRAMMAR]; ある is an auxiliary verb that follows a transitive verb in the **te**-form and expresses the state that resulted from the action.

  EXAMPLE:

  電気がつけてある。

  Denki ga tsuketearu.

  The light has been turned on.
- 寝衣 = 寝巻き **nemaki** sleep-wear
- 着かえる **kikaeru** = 着替える **kigaeru** to change one's clothes
- 臥かしつける = 寝かしつける **nekashi-tsukeru** to lull (a child) to sleep; to put a person to sleep
- 熱を出す **netsu o dasu** to run a fever
- 木の葉 **ko-no-ha** leaves on a tree
- 気丈な **kijō na** stout-hearted; firm
- 甲斐々々しく = 甲斐甲斐しく **kaigaishiku** diligently
- 心の底から **kokoro no soko kara** from the bottom of one's heart
- 挨拶 **aisatsu** greeting
- 言葉 **kotoba** words
- 得…ない **e ... nai** (archaic) not be able to do ...
- 唯 **tada** merely
- うなずく **unazuku** to nod
- (…て) ばかりいる **(... te)-bakari iru** do nothing but ... [GRAMMAR] ばかりいる follows a verb in the **te**-form and expresses that the action is excessive.

  EXAMPLE:

  妹は泣いてばかりいた。

  Imōto wa naite-bakari ita.

  My little sister did nothing but cry.
- 住まる **sumaru** = 住む **sumu** to reside
- 聞き出す **kikidasu** to get information out of a person

■ 麦湯 **mugiyu** = 麦茶 **mugicha** parched barley tea
■ 心配 **shinpai** worry, concern
■ …そうな **… sō na** to appear …

EXAMPLE:
高そうなドレス **takasō na doresu** *a dress that looks expensive*

■ お辞儀 **ojigi** bow
■ 駆けこむ **kakekomu** to rush in
■ …なすって **nasutte** = なさって **nasatte** to do (honorific)
■ お前 **omae** you (derogatory form)
■ いいなすった **iinasutta** = おっしゃった **osshatta**
■ 眼がくらむ = 目がくらむ **me ga kuramu** to become dizzy
■ …ようだ **yō da** It is just like … [GRAMMAR] よう **yō** expresses a simile, although it can also express one's conjecture depending on the context.

EXAMPLE:
まるで雲の上を歩いているようだった。
Marude kumo no ue o aruiteiru yō datta.
It was just like walking on a cloud.

■ …でもしたら **… demo shitara** if such a thing like … happens
■ …つもり **… tsumori** intention, plan [GRAMMAR] つもり follows a verb in the plain form and shows one's intention.

EXAMPLE:
あの車を買うつもりです。
Ano kuruma o kau tsumori desu.
I plan to buy that car.

■ …はしたものの **… wa shita mono no** although …
■ 気をつけておくれでないと **ki o tsukete okure de nai to** = 気をつけてくれないと **ki o tsukete kurenai to** if you won't be careful
■ ほんに **hon ni** = 本当に **hontō ni** truly
■ やがて **yagate** eventually, before long
■ きっとなる **kitto naru** to suddenly become serious
■ すえる **sueru** let something be placed somewhere
■ すくむ **sukumu** to freeze (from fear, etc.)
■ 針 **hari** needle

■ つく **tsuku** to poke

■ こちん **kochin** [MIMETIC] hard, stiff

■ しんしん **shinshin** [MIMETIC] heavily for falling or shining

■ 縁 **en** = 縁側 **engawa** open corridor typical of Japanese-style houses

■ 照りつける **teritsukeru** to shine down on

■ 何んといっても = 何といっても **nan to itte mo** after all is said and done

■ 受取る **uketoru** to receive

■ 知れていました **shireteimashi-ta** was known

■ この世 **konoyo** this world (as opposed to the world of the dead)

■ 妙な **myō na** strange, mysterious

■ 殺す **korosu** to kill

■ 生き残る **ikinokoru** to survive

■ …たんびに **... tanbi ni** = …たびに（…度に） **... tabi ni** every time when ...

■ 恨めしく思う **urameshiku omou** to feel resentful

■ 胸 **mune** chest

■ 動悸 **dōki** palpitation

■ 空… **sora ...** vaguely, somehow, for no reason (preceding an adjective)

Exercises

Select the most appropriate item in the parentheses.

1. うちに着くと、もう妹のために床がとって（い・あり）ました。

2. （おばあさん・M）は妹の世話をしてねかしつけました。

3. おばあさんは若者にお礼を言いましたが、若者は（うなずき・うなずいて）ばかりいました。

4. そして、若者は（心配な・心配）そうに妹を見て、お辞儀をして帰りました。

5. その後、おばあさんはあの時は死ぬ（つもり・はず）であの砂山を駆け上がったといい、私に気をつけなければ本当に困るといいました。

6. おばあさんは若者のうちにお礼のものを（もって・つれて）行きましたが、若者は受けとりませんでした。

7. 今は若者は（どこ・何）にいるか分かりません。

8. おばあさんはもうなくなりました。M は（殺し・殺され）ました。

9. 今でも妹とあの日の話をすると（心配・動悸が）して恐ろしく思います。

Discussion Questions

1. What kind of person was the young man? Why do you think this?

2. Do you think the relationship between the protagonist and his sister changed after that day?

3. What kind of lessons do you think this story can teach us? List as many as you can.

Gauche the Cellist

by Kenji Miyazawa

宮沢賢治 (MIYAZAWA Kenji 1896–1933)
Kenji Miyazawa was born in 1896 in Iwate in northern Japan, to a wealthy family that ran a pawnshop. As a devout Buddhist, he refused to take over his family business and dedicated his life to helping the poor. He studied Agricultural Science at Morioka Agriculture and Forestry College. He was also an artist (painter, cellist and composer), loved opera and classical music, and studied English, German and Esperanto. He died of pneumonia in 1933.

His representative literary works include "Ame ni mo makezu" (雨ニモマケズ), "Chūmon no ōi ryōriten" (注文の多い料理店) *and* "Ginga-tetsudō no yoru" (銀河鉄道の夜). "Serohiki no Gōshu" (セロ弾きのゴーシュ) *was published in 1934, one year after his death.*

✻✻✻ **[PART ONE]** ✻✻✻

Gauche was the person in charge of playing the cello at the town's movie house. However, he was infamous for not being particularly good at it. It wasn't so much that he wasn't good at it, but he was the least talented musician among his colleagues, and so he was always scolded by the conductor.

In the afternoon, everyone was standing in a circle in the dressing room. They were practicing the *Sixth Symphony* for their performance at the next neighborhood concert.

The trumpeter was playing with all his might.

The violinists were playing two melodies, like a two-colored wind.

宮沢賢治

＊＊＊ **[PART ONE]** ＊＊＊

ゴーシュは町の活動写真館でセロを弾く係りでした。けれどもあんまり上手でないという評判でした。上手でないどころではなく実は仲間の楽手のなかではいちばん下手でしたから、いつでも楽長にいじめられるのでした。

ひるすぎみんなは楽屋に円くならんで今度の町の音楽会へ出す第六交響曲の練習をしていました。

トランペットは一生けん命歌っています。

ヴァイオリンも二いろ風のように鳴っています。

クラリネットもボーボーとそれに手伝っています。

ゴーシュも口をりんと結んで眼を皿のようにして楽譜を見つめながらもう一心に弾いています。

にわかにぱたっと楽長が両手を鳴らしました。みんなぴたりと曲をやめてしんとしました。楽長がどなりました。

The clarinetist also joined in with a dark, velvety sound.

Gauche's lips were drawn together in a firm line, and his eyes were as wide as saucers as he concentrated intently on his sheet music while playing.

Suddenly, the conductor clapped his hands together sharply. Everyone quickly stopped playing and fell silent. The conductor yelled, "The cello was late. Let's start again from where it goes 'totiti, tititititi.' Three, two, one!"

Everyone started playing again, from the bit before where they had last stopped. Gauche's face was all red and his forehead was all sweaty, but he finally got past the part that had been pointed out. He continued playing, feeling relieved, but the conductor suddenly clapped his hands again.

"Cello. Your strings aren't tuned right. You're causing a problem. I don't have the extra time to teach you scales."

⁂ [PART TWO] ⁂

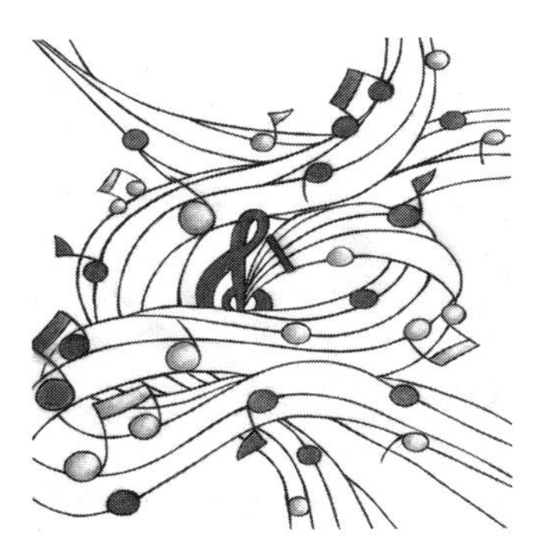

Everyone seemed sympathetic, and they each looked deliberately at their own sheet music and tried plucking at the strings on their own instruments. Gauche hurriedly fixed his strings. This was actually not only Gauche's fault, but the cello's fault as well.

"Let's start from the measure before this one. Three, two, one!"

「セロがおくれた。トォテテ　テテテイ、ここからやり直し。はいっ。」
　みんなは今の所の少し前の所からやり直しました。ゴーシュは顔をまっ赤にして額に汗を出しながらやっといま云われたところを通りました。ほっと安心しながら、つづけて弾いていますと楽長がまた手をぱっと拍ちました。
「セロっ。糸が合わない。困るなあ。ぼくはきみにドレミファを教えてまでいるひまはないんだがなあ。」

✻✻✻ **[PART TWO]** ✻✻✻

みんなは気の毒そうにしてわざとじぶんの譜をのぞき込んだりじぶんの楽器をはじいて見たりしています。ゴーシュはあわてて糸を直しました。これはじつはゴーシュも悪いのですがセロもずいぶん悪いのでした。
「今の前の小節から。はいっ。」
　みんなはまたはじめました。ゴーシュも口をまげて一生けん命です。そしてこんどはかなり進みました。いいあんばいだと思っていると楽長がおどすような形をしてまたぱたっと手を拍ちました。またかとゴーシュはどきっとしましたがありがたいことにはこんどは別の人でした。ゴーシュはそこでさっきじぶんのときみんながしたようにわざとじぶんの譜へ眼を近づけて何か考えるふりをしていました。
「ではすぐ今の次。はいっ。」
　そらと思って弾き出したかと思うといきなり楽長が足をどんと踏んでどなり出しました。
「だめだ。まるでなっていない。このへんは曲の心臓なんだ。それがこんながさがさしたことで。諸君。演奏までもうあと

Everyone started again. Gauche tried his best, his mouth all twisted up. This time, they made considerable progress. But just when he thought that everything was going well, the conductor looked like he was going to scold someone and again clapped his hands sharply. "Again?" Gauche thought, shocked. But thankfully, this time the problem was another person. Gauche stared closely at his sheet music and pretended to think about something else, like everyone had done for him.

"Alright, now we'll go to the next one. Three, two, one!" the conductor said.

As soon as Gauche pulled himself together and started to play, the conductor suddenly stamped his foot and started yelling.

"Terrible. Not right at all. This part is the heart of the piece. Playing it so roughly is unacceptable. Everyone, please. There are only ten days left until the performance. What would it say about our honor if we lost to a band consisting of apprentices from places filled with blacksmiths and sugar shops? You, Gauche—you're really troubling. Your playing has no expression at all. Emotions like anger or joy don't come through in the least. And your playing is never exactly in sync with the other instruments. It's like you're the only one always walking after the others with your shoelaces dragging. It's a real problem. Please try to get it right, because if our splendid Venus Orchestra gets a bad reputation solely because of you, it would be really unfortunate for the other members. Well, that ends practice for today. Go get some rest, and please come back to the orchestra pit at six o'clock sharp."

Everyone bowed. After that, some of them lit cigarettes, and some others left. Gauche, holding his shabby box-like cello, faced the wall and grimaced while tears fell. However, he pulled himself together and started quietly playing today's piece from the beginning, all alone.

十日しかないんだよ。音楽を専門にやっているぼくらがあの金沓鍛冶だの砂糖屋の丁稚なんかの寄り集りに負けてしまったらいったいわれわれの面目はどうなるんだ。おいゴーシュ君。君には困るんだがなあ。表情ということがまるでできてない。怒るも喜ぶも感情というものがさっぱり出ないんだ。それにどうしてもぴたっと外の楽器と合わないもなあ。いつでもきみだけとけた靴のひもを引きずってみんなのあとをついてあるくようなんだ、困るよ、しっかりしてくれないとねえ。光輝あるわが金星音楽団がきみ一人のために悪評をとるようなことでは、みんなへもまったく気の毒だからな。では今日は練習はここまで、休んで六時にはかっきりボックスへ入ってくれ給え。」

　みんなはおじぎをして、それからたばこをくわえてマッチをすったりどこかへ出て行ったりしました。ゴーシュはその粗末な箱みたいなセロをかかえて壁の方へ向いて口をまげてぼろぼろ泪をこぼしましたが、気をとり直してじぶんだけたったひとりいまやったところをはじめからしずかにもいちど弾きはじめました。

＊＊＊ [PART THREE] ＊＊＊

晩遅くゴーシュは何か巨きな黒いものをしょってじぶんの家へ帰ってきました。家といってもそれは町はずれの川ばたにあるこわれた水車小屋で、ゴーシュはそこにたった一人ですんでいて午前は小屋のまわりの小さな畑でトマトの枝をきったり甘藍の虫をひろったりしてひるすぎになるといつも出て行っていたのです。ゴーシュがうちへ入ってあかりをつけるとさっきの黒い包みをあけました。それは何でもない。あの

⁂ [PART THREE] ⁂

Late that night, Gauche returned to his house, carrying something big and black on his back. His so-called "house" was really a run-down water mill in the river valley on the outskirts of town. Gauche lived there all by himself. In the mornings, he trimmed the branches of the tomato plants in the small garden surrounding his shack, and picked off the bugs from the cabbages. He always went out in the afternoons. When he got home, he turned on the light and undid the black wrappings. It was nothing special. It was just his rugged old cello from that evening. Gauche placed it gently on the floor, and suddenly grabbed a cup from the shelf and gulped down water from the bucket.

After that, he shook his head once, sat on a chair, and started playing the music from that afternoon with the energy of a tiger. He flipped the sheet music pages, played, brooded, and played again. After he had played until the end with all his might, he started from the beginning again and again, continuing to play thunderously.

Midnight had already passed, and at the end he didn't even know if he was playing or not; his face was all red and his eyes were completely bloodshot. He looked as if he might pass out at any minute.

At that moment, someone knocked on the door behind him.

"Hauche, are you there?"

Gauche yelled like he was half asleep. Despite that, a large calico cat slipped through the door. Gauche had seen this cat five or six times before.

The cat had brought some half-ripe tomatoes that it had taken from Gauche's garden. The way it was carrying them made them seem really heavy. It put them down in front of Gauche and started to speak.

夕方のごつごつしたセロでした。ゴーシュはそれを床の上にそっと置くと、いきなり棚からコップをとってバケツの水をごくごくのみました。

それから頭を一つふって椅子へかけるとまるで虎みたいな勢でひるの譜を弾きはじめました。譜をめくりながら弾いては考え考えては弾き一生けん命しまいまで行くとまたはじめからなんべんもなんべんもごうごうごうごう弾きつづけました。

夜中もとうにすぎてしまいはもうじぶんが弾いているのかもわからないようになって顔もまっ赤になり眼もまるで血走ってとても物凄い顔つきになりいまにも倒れるかと思うように見えました。

そのとき誰かうしろの扉をとんとんと叩くものがありました。

「ホーシュ君か。」

ゴーシュはねぼけたように叫びました。ところがすうと扉を押してはいって来たのはいままで五六ぺん見たことのある大きな三毛猫でした。

ゴーシュの畑からとった半分熟したトマトをさも重そうに持って来てゴーシュの前におろして云いました。

"Ahh, I'm so tired. Carrying that was really tough."

"What?!" Gauche asked.

"These are a gift. Please, eat them," said the calico cat.

Gauche shouted out his irritation that had been weighing on him since the afternoon.

"And who even asked you to bring tomatoes? Who's to say that I would even eat the food you've given me in the first place? And on top of that, those tomatoes are from my garden. What the hell? You've picked ones that aren't even ripe. I guess you were the one who's been chewing at the tomato stalks and knocking them over till now, right? Get away, damn cat!"

At that, the cat bristled and narrowed its eyes, and said with a smirk, "Sir, getting angry like that is bad for your health. Instead, try playing Schumann's *Träumerei*. I'll listen."

"Such a smart mouth for a cat!" Gauche had become really irritated, and he thought about what to do with the cat for a moment.

"Please, don't be shy. Go ahead, please play. I can't sleep without hearing you play."

"What a smart aleck! What a smart-mouthed wise guy!"

*** [PART FOUR] ***

Gauche's face got all red, and he stamped his feet and yelled like the conductor had done earlier that day. But suddenly, his mood changed. "Well then, I'll play."

For some reason, Gauche locked the door and closed the window, and then he got his cello and put out the light. The moonlight from the waning moon shined in from outside, partially illuminating the room.

"What should I play?"

「ああくたびれた。なかなか運搬はひどいやな。」
「何だと。」ゴーシュがききました。
「これおみやです。たべてください。」三毛猫が云いました。
ゴーシュはひるからのむしゃくしゃを一ぺんにどなりつけました。
「誰がきさまにトマトなど持ってこいと云った。第一おれがきさまらのもってきたものなど食うか。それからそのトマトだっておれの畑のやつだ。何だ。赤くもならないやつをむしって。いままでもトマトの茎をかじったりけちらしたりしたのはおまえだろう。行ってしまえ。ねこめ。」
すると猫は肩をまるくして眼をすぼめてはいましたが口のあたりでにやにやわらって云いました。
「先生、そうお怒りになっちゃ、おからだにさわります。それよりシューマンのトロメライをひいてごらんなさい。きいてあげますから。」
「生意気なことを云うな。ねこのくせに。」
セロ弾きはしゃくにさわってこのねこのやつどうしてくれようとしばらく考えました。
「いやご遠慮はありません。どうぞ。わたしはどうも先生の音楽をきかないとねむられないんです。」
「生意気だ。生意気だ。生意気だ。」

✻✻✻ **[PART FOUR]** ✻✻✻

ゴーシュはすっかりまっ赤になってひるま楽長のしたように足ぶみしてどなりましたがにわかに気を変えて云いました。
「では弾くよ。」

"*Träumerei*, composed by the romantic Schumann," the cat said, wiping its mouth and assuming a calm and collected look.

"I see. Is *Träumerei* like this?"

First, the cello player tore a handkerchief and stuffed it in his ears for some reason. Then, he started playing the piece, "Tiger Hunting in India" thunderously.

The cat listened for a while with its head tilted, but then it suddenly blinked several times and quickly jumped toward the door. The cat suddenly hit its body against the door with a bang, but the door didn't open. The cat got flustered as if that was the biggest failure of its life, and sparks appeared from its eyes and forehead. Then, because the sparks started flying from both its whiskers and its nose, the cat felt ticklish; and for a while, it made a face that looked like it was about to sneeze. Then it started trotting around, as if it couldn't stand it anymore. Gauche was thoroughly amused by this and played with more and more vigor.

"Sir, that's enough now. That's enough. For heaven's sake, please stop. I'll never take your baton or anything else ever again."

"Be quiet. This is the part where they catch the tiger."

The cat looked like it was in pain and jumped around and backed up against the wall, and after a while its body glowed blue. By the end, the cat was running around and around Gauche like a windmill.

ゴーシュは何と思ったか扉にかぎをかって窓もみんなしめてしまい、それからセロをとりだしてあかしを消しました。すると外から二十日過ぎの月のひかりが室のなかへ半分ほどはいってきました。

「何をひけと。」

「トロメライ、ロマチックシューマン作曲。」猫は口を拭いて澄まして云いました。

「そうか。トロメライというのはこういうのか。」

セロ弾きは何と思ったかまずはんけちを引きさいてじぶんの耳の穴へぎっしりつめました。それからまるで嵐のような勢で「印度の虎狩」という譜を弾きはじめました。

すると猫はしばらく首をまげて聞いていましたがいきなりパチパチパチッと眼をしたかと思うとぱっと扉の方へ飛びのきました。そしていきなりどんと扉へからだをぶっつけましたが扉はあきませんでした。猫はさあこれはもう一生一代の失敗をしたという風にあわてだして眼や額からぱちぱち火花を出しました。するとこんどは口のひげからも鼻からも出ましたから猫はくすぐったがってしばらくくしゃみをするような顔をしてそれからまたさあこうしてはいられないぞというようにはせあるきだしました。ゴーシュはすっかり面白くなってますます勢よくやり出しました。

「先生もうたくさんです。たくさんですよ。ご生ですからやめてください。これからもう先生のタクトなんかとりませんから。」

「だまれ。これから虎をつかまえる所だ。」

猫はくるしがってはねあがってまわったり壁にからだをくっつけたりしましたが壁についたあとはしばらく青くひかる

Since Gauche was also getting dizzy, he finally stopped as he said, "Fine, I'll stop here."

And as if nothing had happened, the cat said, "Sir, there was something the matter with tonight's performance."

Gauche felt irritated again, and casually took out a cigar, holding it to his mouth. He took out a match and said, "How are you? Are you feeling sick? Stick out your tongue."

The cat stuck out its long, sharp tongue mockingly.

"Haha, it got a bit rough, didn't it?" As he said that, Gauche suddenly struck the match on the cat's tongue, and lit his cigar with it. The cat was so surprised that it waved its tongue around like a windmill and went to the door, thumping its head against it repeatedly trying to create a way out, staggering after each thump.

Gauche watched it for a while in amusement, but then he said, "I'll let you go. Don't come back anymore. Idiot."

The cellist opened the door, and the cat ran away like the wind blowing through the reeds. Gauche laughed a little at the sight. After that, finally feeling refreshed, Gauche fell fast asleep.

⁂ [PART FIVE] ⁂

The next night, Gauche came home again, carrying the cello that was wrapped in black on his back. And, just like last night, he gulped down water and started steadily playing the cello. Before long, midnight had passed; and then one o'clock, and then two o'clock had passed, too.

But Gauche had not stopped playing yet. Soon, he did not even know what time it was, or if he was even playing. As he was playing loudly, a knocking sound came from the attic.

のでした。しまいは猫はまるで風車のようにぐるぐるぐるぐるゴーシュをまわりました。
ゴーシュもすこしぐるぐるして来ましたので、
「さあこれで許してやるぞ」と云いながらようようやめました。
すると猫もけろりとして
「先生、こんやの演奏はどうかしてますね。」と云いました。
セロ弾きはまたぐっとしゃくにさわりましたが何気ない風で巻たばこを一本だして口にくわえそれからマッチを一本とって
「どうだい。工合をわるくしないかい。舌を出してごらん。」
猫はばかにしたように尖った長い舌をベロリと出しました。
「ははあ、少し荒れたね。」セロ弾きは云いながらいきなりマッチを舌でシュッとすってじぶんのたばこへつけました。さあ猫は愕いたの何の舌を風車のようにふりまわしながら入り口の扉へ行って頭でどんとぶっつかってはよろよろとしてまた戻って来てどんとぶっつかってはよろよろまた戻って来てまたぶっつかってはよろよろにげみちをこさえようとしました。
ゴーシュはしばらく面白そうに見ていましたが
「出してやるよ。もう来るなよ。ばか。」
セロ弾きは扉をあけて猫が風のように萱のなかを走って行くのを見てちょっとわらいました。それから、やっとせいせいしたというようにぐっすりねむりました。

✻✻✻ [PART FIVE] ✻✻✻

次の晩もゴーシュがまた黒いセロの包みをかついで帰ってきました。そして水をごくごくのむとそっくりゆうべのとおりぐんぐんセロを弾きはじめました。十二時は間もなく過ぎ一時も

“Cat! You still haven’t learned your lesson?”

As he shouted that, a gray bird suddenly dropped down from a hole in the ceiling and landed with a plop. Looking at the creature on the floor, Gauche saw that it was a cuckoo.

“And now a bird comes, too? What do you want?” Gauche asked.

“I want to learn music,” the cuckoo said calmly.

“Music, you say? Isn’t the only song you can sing ‘cuckoo, cuckoo’?” Gauche said while laughing.

At that, the bird became very serious.

“Yes, that’s what I’m talking about. But it’s difficult,” it said.

“Difficult? You guys sing so much, the way you sing can’t be that hard to do.”

“Even so, it’s hard. For example, the ways that I sing ‘cuckoo’ like this and ‘cuckoo’ like that sound completely different, right?”

“No, they don’t.”

“Then you don’t understand. To us cuckoos, if we say ‘cuckoo’ ten thousand times, each one of those times sounds different.”

“Fine, have it your way. If you knew that much about it, then you didn’t have to come into my house, did you?”

“But I want to be able to sing scales accurately.”

“Forget scales.”

“I definitely need to know how to do it before I go abroad.”

“Forget going abroad.”

“Sir, please teach me scales. I’ll sing by following your lead.”

“You’re so annoying. Fine, I’ll play it for you, but only three times. After that, quickly go right home.”

Gauche picked up his cello, tuned the strings, and played do-re-mi-fa-sol-la-ti-do. The cuckoo flapped its wings urgently.

すぎ二時もすぎてもゴーシュはまだやめませんでした。それからもう何時だかもわからず弾いているかもわからずごうごうやっていますと誰か屋根裏をこっこっと叩くものがあります。

「猫、まだこりないのか。」

ゴーシュが叫びますといきなり天井の穴からぽろんと音がして一疋の灰いろの鳥が降りて来ました。床へとまったのを見るとそれはかっこうでした。

「鳥まで来るなんて。何の用だ。」ゴーシュが云いました。

「音楽を教わりたいのです。」かっこう鳥はすまして云いました。

ゴーシュは笑って

「音楽だと。おまえの歌は、かっこう、かっこうというだけじゃあないか。」

するとかっこうが大へんまじめに

「ええ、それなんです。けれどもむずかしいですからねえ。」と云いました。

「むずかしいもんか。おまえたちのはたくさん啼くのがひどいだけで、なきようは何でもないじゃないか。」

「ところがそれがひどいんです。たとえばかっこうとこうなくのとかっこうとこうなくのとでは聞いていてもよほどちがうでしょう。」

「ちがわないね。」

「ではあなたにはわからないんです。わたしらのなかまならかっこうと一万云えば一万みんなちがうんです。」

「勝手だよ。そんなにわかってるなら何もおれの処へ来なくてもいいではないか。」

「ところが私はドレミファを正確にやりたいんです。」

「ドレミファもくそもあるか。」

“Wrong, wrong. Not like that.”

“You’re so bossy! Fine then, you do it.”

“Like this.” The cuckoo bent down and prepared itself before letting out one cry of “cuckoo!”

“What was that? Was that your scale? In that case, scales and the *Sixth Symphony* must be exactly the same for cuckoos!”

“They are different.”

“How are they different then?”

“We have a difficult piece where we have to repeat ‘cuckoo’ over and over.”

“In other words, like this?” The cellist took his cello again and played what sounded like ‘cuckoo, cuckoo, cuckoo, cuckoo, cuckoo’ continuously.

The cuckoo took great pleasure in this and sung along with the cello, its body bent down while crying “cuckoo, cuckoo, cuckoo, cuckoo,” with all its might.

When Gauche’s hand eventually started hurting, he stopped as he said, “Alright, that’s enough.” When the cuckoo heard that, it looked upset and disappointed; it kept singing for a little while, but finally it cried “cuckoo, cuckoo, coo, coo, coo” and stopped.

「ええ、外国へ行く前にぜひ一度いるんです。」
「外国もくそもあるか。」
「先生どうかドレミファを教えてください。わたしはついてうたいますから。」
「うるさいなあ。そら三べんだけ弾いてやるからすんだらさっさと帰るんだぞ。」
ゴーシュはセロを取り上げてボロンボロンと糸を合わせてドレミファソラシドとひきました。するとかっこうはあわてて羽をばたばたしました。
「ちがいます、ちがいます。そんなんでないんです。」
「うるさいなあ。ではおまえやってごらん。」
「こうですよ。」かっこうはからだをまえに曲げてしばらく構えてから「かっこう」と一つなきました。
「何だい。それがドレミファかい。おまえたちには、それではドレミファも第六交響楽も同じなんだな。」
「それはちがいます。」
「どうちがうんだ。」
「むずかしいのはこれをたくさん続けたのがあるんです。」
「つまりこうだろう。」セロ弾きはまたセロをとって、かっこうかっこうかっこうかっこうかっこうとつづけてひきました。
するとかっこうはたいへんよろこんで途中からかっこうかっこうかっこうかっこうとついて叫びました。それもう一生けん命からだをまげていつまでも叫ぶのです。
ゴーシュはとうとう手が痛くなって
「こら、いいかげんにしないか。」と云いながらやめました。するとかっこうは残念そうに眼をつりあげてまだしばらくないていましたがやっと

*** [PART SIX] ***

Gauche, having gotten thoroughly angry, said, "Now bird, if you've done what you wanted to do, go home!"

"Please, play it one more time. Your playing looked good, but it sounded a little off."

"What? I'm not the one being taught by you! Go home!"

"Please, only once more. Please." The cuckoo bowed its head repeatedly.

"Fine. This is the absolute last time."

Gauche prepared his bow. The cuckoo breathed out a lone "coo" and bowed again, saying,

"Then, please play as long as possible."

"Such a nuisance," said Gauche, and he started playing with a wry smile on his face. And at that, the cuckoo became very serious again, and bent down while crying "cuckoo, cuckoo" with all its might. At first Gauche was annoyed, but as he kept playing, he got the feeling that the cuckoo was more in tune with the scales than he was. The more he played, the more he felt that the cuckoo was better than him.

"If I don't stop doing this kind of stupid thing, won't I become a bird too?" said Gauche, and he abruptly stopped playing the cello.

And at that, the cuckoo staggered as if it had been hit on the head; it cried "cuckoo, cuckoo, coo coo coo" like it had done a while before, and then it stopped. It then looked at Gauche reproachfully and said, "Why did you stop? We cuckoos, even those of us with no self-confidence, will keep crying until our throats bleed," it said.

"You think you're such hot stuff. How long can I keep going along with this kind of monkey business? Get out, now! Look, isn't dawn breaking?" Gauche said, pointing to the window.

「……かっこうかくうかっかっかっかっか」と云ってやめました。

＊＊＊ [PART SIX] ＊＊＊

ゴーシュがすっかりおこってしまって、

「こらとり、もう用が済んだらかえれ」と云いました。

「どうかもういっぺん弾いてください。あなたのはいいようだけれどもすこしちがうんです。」

「何だと、おれがきさまに教わってるんではないんだぞ。帰らんか。」

「どうかたったもう一ぺんおねがいです。どうか。」かっこうは頭を何べんもこんこん下げました。

「ではこれっきりだよ。」

ゴーシュは弓をかまえました。かっこうは「くっ」とひとつ息をして

「ではなるべく永くおねがいいたします。」といってまた一つおじぎをしました。

「いやになっちまうなあ。」ゴーシュはにが笑いしながら弾きはじめました。するとかっこうはまたまるで本気になって「かっこうかっこうかっこう」とからだをまげてじつに一生けん命叫びました。ゴーシュははじめはむしゃくしゃしていましたがいつまでもつづけて弾いているうちにふっと何だかこれは鳥の方がほんとうのドレミファにはまっているかなという気がしてきました。どうも弾けば弾くほどかっこうの方がいいような気がするのでした。

「えい、こんなばかなことしていたらおれは鳥になってしまうんじゃないか。」とゴーシュはいきなりぴたりとセロをやめました。

The eastern sky was turning faintly silver, and the dark clouds were steadily traveling northward.

"Then, play until the sun rises, please. One more time. Just a little more," the cuckoo said, bowing its head again.

"Shut up! You're so conceited! Stupid bird. If you don't leave, I'll pluck your feathers and eat you for breakfast," Gauche said, and stamped on the floor with a thump.

Suddenly, the cuckoo flew toward the window as if it were surprised, but it hit its head violently against the glass and fell to the floor.

"What the hell, stupid bird, hitting the glass!" Gauche hastily stood up and tried to open the window, but this window had always been hard to open. While Gauche kept rattling the window frame, the cuckoo suddenly ran into the window again and fell down. As he looked, Gauche noticed that the base of its beak was bleeding a little.

"I'm opening the window for you right now, so wait a minute!" When Gauche had finally opened the window about two inches, the cuckoo got up and suddenly flew with all its might, staring straight through the window at the eastern sky, as if it were thinking that this time it would get through at all costs. Of course, this time the cuckoo collided with the glass harder than before and fell down. It didn't move for a while. Gauche reached out his hand to try and catch the bird to let it out the door,

するとかっこうはどしんと頭を叩かれたようにふらふらっとしてそれからまたさっきのように

「かっこうかっこうかっこうかっかっかっかっかっ」と云ってやめました。それから恨めしそうにゴーシュを見て

「なぜやめたんですか。ぼくらならどんな意気地ないやつでものどから血が出るまでは叫ぶんですよ。」と云いました。

「何を生意気な。こんなばかなまねをいつまでしていられるか。もう出て行け。見ろ。夜があけるんじゃないか。」ゴーシュは窓を指さしました。

東のそらがぼうっと銀いろになってそこをまっ黒な雲が北の方へどんどん走っています。

「ではお日さまの出るまでどうぞ。もう一ぺん。ちょっとですから。」かっこうはまた頭を下げました。

「黙れっ。いい気になって。このばか鳥め。出て行かんとむしって朝飯に食ってしまうぞ。」ゴーシュはどんと床をふみました。

するとかっこうはにわかにびっくりしたようにいきなり窓をめがけて飛び立ちました。そして硝子にはげしく頭をぶっつけてばたっと下へ落ちました。

「何だ、硝子へばかだなあ。」ゴーシュはあわてて立って窓をあけようとしましたが元来この窓はそんなにいつでもするする開く窓ではありませんでした。ゴーシュが窓のわくをしきりにがたがたしているうちにまたかっこうがばっとぶっつかって下へ落ちました。見ると嘴のつけねからすこし血が出ています。

「いまあけてやるから待っていろったら。」ゴーシュがやっと二寸ばかり窓をあけたとき、かっこうは起きあがって何が何でもこんどこそというようにじっと窓の向うの東のそらを

but suddenly, the cuckoo opened its eyes and jumped back. It looked as if it were going to fly toward the glass again. Without thinking, Gauche raised his leg and kicked the window. Two or three panes of glass broke into pieces with a loud crash, and the window frame fell outside. The cuckoo flew out the now-empty window like an arrow, and it kept flying straight until it finally disappeared from view. Gauche looked outside for a while, astonished. Then he collapsed in the corner of the room and fell asleep.

⁂ **[PART SEVEN]** ⁂

The next night, Gauche played the cello again until midnight, wearing himself out. He drank a cup of water, and again there was a knock at the door.

Gauche decided that tonight, no matter what came, he would threaten it from the beginning and drive it away just as he had done with the cuckoo the night before. While he was waiting for it, still holding the cup, the door opened a little and a baby raccoon came in. Gauche then opened the door a little wider and yelled, stamping his foot, "Hey raccoon, you ever heard of raccoon soup?"

At that, the baby raccoon gave him a dim look and promptly sat on the floor, tilting his head as if he didn't quite understand. After a moment, he said, "I'm not familiar with raccoon soup."

Looking at his face, Gauche almost burst out laughing in spite of himself. Trying very hard to make a scary face, he said, "Then I'll tell you. Raccoon soup is made with raccoons like you, mixed with cabbage and salt, and it's boiled up for me to eat."

みつめて、あらん限りの力をこめた風でぱっと飛びたちました。もちろんこんどは前よりひどく硝子につきあたってかっこうは下へ落ちたまましばらく身動きもしませんでした。つかまえてドアから飛ばしてやろうとゴーシュが手を出しましたらいきなりかっこうは眼をひらいて飛びのきました。そしてまたガラスへ飛びつきそうにするのです。ゴーシュは思わず足を上げて窓をばっとけりました。ガラスは二三枚物すごい音して砕け窓はわくのまま外へ落ちました。そのがらんとなった窓のあとをかっこうが矢のように外へ飛びだしました。そしてもうどこまでもどこまでもまっすぐに飛んで行ってとうとう見えなくなってしまいました。ゴーシュはしばらく呆れたように外を見ていましたが、そのまま倒れるように室のすみへころがって睡ってしまいました。

✻✻✻ [PART SEVEN] ✻✻✻

次の晩もゴーシュは夜中すぎまでセロを弾いてつかれて水を一杯のんでいますと、また扉をこつこつ叩くものがあります。

今夜は何が来てもゆうべのかっこうのようにはじめからおどかして追い払ってやろうと思ってコップをもったまま待ち構えて居りますと、扉がすこしあいて一疋の狸の子がはいってきました。ゴーシュはそこでその扉をもう少し広くひらいて置いてどんと足をふんで、

「こら、狸、おまえは狸汁ということを知っているかっ。」

とどなりました。すると狸の子はぼんやりした顔をしてきちんと床へ座ったままどうもわからないというように首をまげて考えていましたが、しばらくたって

The baby raccoon again looked puzzled, but curious, and said, "But my father told me that since you are a nice person who is not scary, I should go and learn from you."

At that, Gauche finally burst into laughter. "What kind of lesson did he say? Aren't I busy? Besides, I'm sleepy."

The baby raccoon suddenly took a step forward with a new vigor. "I'm in charge of playing the small drum, so he told me to go and ask you to let me play alongside your cello."

"You don't have a small drum anywhere, do you?"

"Look, here," the baby raccoon said, and he took two sticks out from behind his back.

"What will you do with those?"

"Now, please play '*The Happy Coachman*'."

"Is that a jazz piece?"

"Ah, here's the sheet music," said the baby raccoon, taking out one piece of sheet music from behind his back. Gauche took it and burst out laughing.

"Hah! This is a weird piece. Alright, I'll start. Are you going to play the drum?" Gauche glanced at the baby raccoon, wondering what he was going to do, and started playing.

「狸汁ってぼく知らない。」と云いました。ゴーシュはその顔を見て思わず吹き出そうとしましたが、まだ無理に恐い顔をして、

「では教えてやろう。狸汁というのはな。おまえのような狸をな、キャベジや塩とまぜてくたくたと煮ておれさまの食うようにしたものだ。」と云いました。すると狸の子はまたふしぎそうに

「だってぼくのお父さんがね、ゴーシュさんはとてもいい人でこわくないから行って習えと云ったよ。」と云いました。そこでゴーシュもとうとう笑い出してしまいました。

「何を習えと云ったんだ。おれはいそがしいんじゃないか。それに睡いんだよ。」

狸の子は俄に勢がついたように一足前へ出ました。

「ぼくは小太鼓の係りでねえ。セロへ合わせてもらって来いと云われたんだ。」

「どこにも小太鼓がないじゃないか。」

「そら、これ」狸の子はせなかから棒きれを二本出しました。

「それでどうするんだ。」

「ではね、『愉快な馬車屋』を弾いてください。」

「なんだ愉快な馬車屋ってジャズか。」

「ああこの譜だよ。」狸の子はせなかからまた一枚の譜をとり出しました。ゴーシュは手にとってわらい出しました。

「ふう、変な曲だなあ。よし、さあ弾くぞ。おまえは小太鼓を叩くのか。」ゴーシュは狸の子がどうするのかと思ってちらちらそっちを見ながら弾きはじめました。

すると狸の子は棒をもってセロの駒の下のところを拍子をとってぽんぽん叩きはじめました。それがなかなかうまいの

The baby raccoon started tapping under the bridge of the cello, keeping tempo. It sounded pretty good, so Gauche thought it was amusing.

When they reached the end, the baby raccoon tilted his head in thought for a little while.

After that, he spoke up, as if he had finally come to a conclusion.

"There's a delay when you play the second string. You come in later than I expected. So I feel like I stumbled a bit."

Gauche was taken aback. It's true that since last night, Gauche had had the feeling that the second string was late, no matter how quickly he played it.

"Well, you could say that. This cello is pretty bad," said Gauche sadly. The raccoon looked sympathetic and thought for a while.

"I wonder where the problem is. Could you play it for me one more time?"

"Sure thing." Gauche started playing, and the baby raccoon tapped on the cello like before, sometimes bending his head and putting his ear against the cello. And when they reached the end, the eastern sky was growing brighter again.

"Oh, dawn is breaking. Thanks a lot." The baby raccoon hurriedly took the sheet music and sticks, fastened them back behind his back with a rubber band, bowed a few times, and quickly went outside.

For a while, Gauche breathed in the wind that was coming through the window that had been broken last night with a dim look on his face, and then he hurriedly slipped into bed in order to get his strength back before going into town.

で弾いているうちにゴーシュはこれは面白(おもしろ)いぞと思いました。

おしまいまでひいてしまうと狸の子はしばらく首をまげて考(かんが)えました。

それからやっと考えついたというように云いました。

「ゴーシュさんはこの二番目(にばんめ)の糸(いと)をひくときはきたいに遅(おく)れるねえ。なんだかぼくがつまずくようになるよ。」

ゴーシュははっとしました。たしかにその糸はどんなに手早(てばや)く弾いてもすこしたってからでないと音(おと)が出(で)ないような気(き)がゆうべからしていたのでした。

「いや、そうかもしれない。このセロは悪(わる)いんだよ。」とゴーシュはかなしそうに云いました。すると狸は気(き)の毒(どく)そうにしてまたしばらく考(かんが)えていましたが

「どこが悪いんだろうなあ。ではもう一ぺん弾いてくれますか。」

「いいとも弾くよ。」ゴーシュははじめました。狸の子はさっきのようにとんとん叩きながら時々(ときどき)頭(あたま)をまげてセロに耳(みみ)をつけるようにしました。そしておしまいまで来たときは今夜(こんや)もまた東(ひがし)がぼうと明(あか)るくなっていました。

「ああ夜(よ)が明(あ)けたぞ。どうもありがとう。」狸の子は大へんあわてて譜や棒きれをせなかへしょってゴムテープでぱちんととめておじぎを二つ三つすると急(いそ)いで外(そと)へ出て行ってしまいました。

ゴーシュはぼんやりしてしばらくゆうべのこわれたガラスからはいってくる風(かぜ)を吸(す)っていましたが、町(まち)へ出て行くまで睡(ねむ)って元気(げんき)をとり戻(もど)そうと急(いそ)いでねどこへもぐり込(こ)みました。

*** [PART EIGHT] ***

The next evening, Gauche played his cello all night again, and as dawn was approaching, he unintentionally dozed off holding his sheet music. Again, there was a knock at the door. It was hard to hear, but since visitors had come every night, Gauche immediately noticed it and said, "Come in." A field mouse came in through the crack of the door. She darted toward Gauche with an incredibly small baby mouse following her. The baby mouse was as tiny as an eraser, and Gauche couldn't help but laugh.

The field mouse looked around restlessly as she approached him, wondering what Gauche was laughing about. She placed an unripe chestnut before him and gave him a proper bow.

"Sir, my child is sick and it looks like he will die soon. Please cure him with your mercy," she said.

"You want me to act as a doctor? No way," Gauche said, slightly offended. At that, the mother mouse looked down and was silent for a while. She then spoke again, boldly.

"Sir, that's a lie. Do you not skillfully cure everyone's illnesses every day?"

"I don't know what you're talking about."

＊＊＊ [PART EIGHT] ＊＊＊

次の晩もゴーシュは夜通しセロを弾いて明方近く思わずつかれて楽譜をもったままうとうとしていますとまた誰か扉をこつこつと叩くものがあります。それもまるで聞えるか聞えないかの位でしたが毎晩のことなのでゴーシュはすぐ聞きつけて

「おはいり。」と云いました。すると戸のすきまからはいって来たのは一ぴきの野ねずみでした。そして大へんちいさなこどもをつれてちょろちょろとゴーシュの前へ歩いてきました。そのまた野ねずみのこどもときたらまるでけしごむのくらいしかないのでゴーシュはおもわずわらいました。すると野ねずみは何をわらわれたろうというようにきょろきょろしながらゴーシュの前に来て、青い栗の実を一つぶ前においてちゃんとおじぎをして云いました。

「先生、この児があんばいがわるくて死にそうでございますが先生お慈悲になおしてやってくださいまし。」

「おれが医者などやれるもんか。」ゴーシュはすこしむっとして云いました。すると野ねずみのお母さんは下を向いてしばらくだまっていましたがまた思い切ったように云いました。

「先生、それはうそでございます、先生は毎日あんなに上手にみんなの病気をなおしておいでになるではありませんか。」

「何のことだかわからんね。」

「だって先生、先生のおかげで、兎さんのおばあさんもなおりましたし狸さんのお父さんもなおりましたしあんな意地悪のみみずくまでなおしていただいたのにこの子ばかりお助けをいただけないとはあんまり情ないことでございます。」

"Thanks to you, the rabbit's grandmother and the raccoon's father were cured, and you even cured the mean horned owl. My child is the only one you won't help. How uncaring."

"Hey now, there must be some kind of misunderstanding. I've never cured any horned owl. Although, last night, a baby raccoon came and performed like a member of the orchestra. Haha!" Gauche felt a bit silly thinking about it, and laughed while looking down at the little mouse.

And then, the mother mouse burst into tears.

"Ah, it would have been better if my child had gotten sick earlier. You have been playing so loudly until a little while ago, but right when my child gets sick, you stop playing and won't play no matter how much I ask you to. How unfortunate my child is!"

Gauche was surprised and exclaimed, "What, are you saying that whenever I play the cello, I cure animals like the owl and rabbit? How do you figure that?"

The field mouse rubbed her eyes with one hand and said, "Yes, if we, the animals around here, get sick, we go under your floor to get cured."

"And then you're all healed?"

"Yes. Our blood circulates better, and some of us feel better right away, while others recover after they return home."

"Is that right? The sound of my cello vibrates through the floor, and that serves as a massage that cures your illnesses? Alright, I got it. I'll play for you."

Gauche tuned the strings for a bit and then suddenly picked up the baby mouse and put him through the hole into the cello.

"I will go with my child. I'd follow him to any hospital," the mother mouse said, jumping at the cello hysterically.

「おいおい、それは何かの間ちがいだよ。おれはみみずくの病気なんどなおしてやったことはないからな。もっとも狸の子はゆうべ来て楽隊のまねをして行ったがね。はは ん。」ゴーシュは呆れてその子ねずみを見おろしてわらいました。

すると野鼠のお母さんは泣きだしてしまいました。

「ああこの児はどうせ病気になるならもっと早くなればよかった。さっきまであれ位ごうごうと鳴らしておいでになったのに、病気になるといっしょにぴたっと音がとまってもうあとはいくらおねがいしても鳴らしてくださらないなんて。何てふしあわせな子どもだろう。」

ゴーシュはびっくりして叫びました。

「何だと、ぼくがセロを弾けばみみずくや兎の病気がなおると。どういうわけだ。それは。」

野ねずみは眼を片手でこすりこすり云いました。

「はい、ここらのものは病気になるとみんな先生のおうちの床下にはいって療すのでございます。」

「すると療るのか。」

「はい。からだ中とても血のまわりがよくなって大へんいい気持ちですぐ療る方もあればうちへ帰ってから療る方もあります。」

「ああそうか。おれのセロの音がごうごうひびくと、それがあんまの代りになっておまえたちの病気がなおるというのか。よし。わかったよ。やってやろう。」ゴーシュはちょっとギウギウと糸を合せてそれからいきなりのねずみのこどもをつまんでセロの孔から中へ入れてしまいました。

「わたしもいっしょについて行きます。どこの病院でもそうですから。」おっかさんの野ねずみはきちがいのようになってセロに飛びつきました。

"You want to go in too?" Gauche tried to put the mother mouse through the hole in the cello, but only half of her head would fit.

*** [PART NINE] ***

As she thrashed about, she cried out to her child, "Are you okay in there? Did you land safely with your feet together like I always taught you to?"

"Yes, I landed fine," the baby mouse answered from inside the bottom of the cello, with a small voice that sounded just like a mosquito.

"It'll be okay, so no crying," Gauche said. Gauche put the mother mouse down, got his bow, and began to loudly play some rhapsody or another. The mother mouse listened to the sound, looking really worried; but finally, as if she couldn't stand it anymore, she cried, "That's enough. Please get him out!"

"What, is this enough?" Gauche tilted the cello and put his hand near the hole, waiting. And before long, the baby mouse came out. Gauche put him down silently. His eyes were shut, and he kept trembling and shivering.

"How was it? Are you okay? How do you feel?"

The baby mouse did not give any reply, and he still had his eyes closed and kept trembling and shivering for a little while, but suddenly he got up and started running.

"Ah, it worked! Thank you, thank you!" The mother mouse also started running around together with her child, and soon approached Gauche and bowed repeatedly, saying "thank you, thank you" about ten times.

Gauche felt somewhat sorry for them and asked, "Hey, do you eat bread?"

「おまえさんもはいるかね。」セロ弾きはおっかさんの野ねずみをセロの孔からくぐしてやろうとしましたが顔が半分しかはいりませんでした。

＊＊＊ [PART NINE] ＊＊＊

野ねずみはばたばたしながら中のこどもに叫びました。

「おまえそこはいいかい。落ちるときいつも教えるように足をそろえてうまく落ちたかい。」

「いい。うまく落ちた。」こどものねずみはまるで蚊のような小さな声でセロの底で返事しました。

「大丈夫さ。だから泣き声出すなというんだ。」ゴーシュはおっかさんのねずみを下におろしてそれから弓をとって何とかラプソディとかいうものをごうごうがあがあ弾きました。するとおっかさんのねずみはいかにも心配そうにその音の工合をきいていましたがとうとうこらえ切れなくなったふうで

「もう沢山です。どうか出してやってください。」と云いました。

「なあんだ、これでいいのか。」ゴーシュはセロをまげて孔のところに手をあてて待っていましたら間もなくこどものねずみが出てきました。ゴーシュは、だまってそれをおろしてやりました。見るとすっかり目をつぶってぶるぶるぶるぶるふるえていました。

「どうだったの。いいかい。気分は。」

こどものねずみはすこしもへんじもしないでまだしばらく眼をつぶったままぶるぶるぶるぶるふるえていましたがにわかに起きあがって走りだした。

At this, the field mice looked around restlessly as if they were surprised, and the mother mouse said, "No, well, bread is… I've heard it's made by kneading wheat flour and steaming it, and it swells up all plump and soft, and it sounds delicious. But even if it's not, we have never been in your cupboards, not to mention that you've already helped us this much already, how could we come to carry it?"

"No, it's not like that. I just asked if you eat bread. So, you do eat it. Wait a minute, I'll get some for your sick child."

Gauche put his cello down on the floor, tore off a tiny piece of bread from the cupboard, and put it down in front of the mice.

The mouse began crying and laughing like a complete fool, bowing over and over. She carefully held the cherished piece of bread in her mouth and left, with her child going on ahead.

"Ahh, talking to mice is tiring." Gauche flopped down on his bed and soon fell fast asleep.

⁂ [PART TEN] ⁂

It was the sixth night after that. The members of the Venus Orchestra were all coming back from the stage one after another, their cheeks glowing as they headed for the back room of the town hall, each holding their instruments. They had successfully performed the *Sixth Symphony*. In the hall, the sound of thunderous applause still continued. The conductor was slowly walking around everyone with his hands in his pockets, as if he didn't care about the applause, but he was actually very happy. Everyone was lighting their cigarettes and putting their instruments back in their cases.

「ああよくなったんだ。ありがとうございます。ありがとうございます。」おっかさんのねずみもいっしょに走っていましたが、まもなくゴーシュの前に来てしきりにおじぎをしながら
「ありがとうございます。ありがとうございます。」と十ばかり云いました。
ゴーシュは何がなかあいそうになって
「おい、おまえたちはパンはたべるのか。」とききました。
すると野鼠はびっくりしたようにきょろきょろあたりを見まわしてから
「いえ、もうおパンというものは小麦の粉をこねたりむしたりしてこしらえたものでふくふく膨らんでいておいしいものなそうでございますが、そうでなくても私どもはおうちの戸棚へなど参ったこともございませんし、ましてこれ位お世話になりながらどうしてそれを運びになんど参れましょう。」と云いました。
「いや、そのことではないんだ。ただたべるのかときいたんだ。ではたべるんだな。ちょっと待てよ。その腹の悪いこどもへやるからな。」
ゴーシュはセロを床へ置いて戸棚からパンを一つまみむしって野ねずみの前へ置きました。
野ねずみはもうまるでばかのようになって泣いたり笑ったりおじぎをしたりしてから大じそうにそれをくわえてこどもをさきに立てて外へ出て行きました。
「あああ。鼠と話するのもなかなかつかれるぞ。」ゴーシュはねどこへどっかり倒れてすぐぐうぐうねむってしまいました。

The clapping in the hall was never-ending. It was gradually getting louder, like a terrifying roar that could not be stopped. The MC, who was wearing a big white ribbon on his chest, came in and said, "They're calling for an encore. Could you just perform something short for them?"

The conductor answered definitively, "No, we can't. After giving such a grand performance, nothing we go out and play now would be satisfying for us."

"Then, Mr. Conductor, please go out and say a few words."

"No, I can't. Hey Gauche, go out and play something for them."

"Me?" Gauche asked, taken aback.

"Yes, you," the first chair violin said, suddenly raising his head.

"Come on, please go," the conductor said. Everyone else thrust the cello into Gauche's hands, opened the door, and suddenly pushed him out on stage. When Gauche stepped onto the stage embarrassedly, holding his cello with the hole in it, the audience clapped even louder, as if to say "There, look at him!" Someone even shouted "Wow!"

"How far will they go to make fun of me? Okay, just watch. I'll play 'Tiger Hunting in India' for them." Once Gauche had thoroughly calmed down, he went to the center of the stage.

And just like when that cat had come, he played "Tiger Hunting in India" with the vigor of an angry elephant. Nevertheless, the audience

✻✻✻ [PART TEN] ✻✻✻

それから六日目の晩でした。金星音楽団の人たちは町の公会堂のホールの裏にある控室へみんなぱっと顔をほてらしてめいめい楽器をもって、ぞろぞろホールの舞台から引きあげて来ました。首尾よく第六交響曲を仕上げたのです。ホールでは拍手の音がまだ嵐のように鳴って居ります。楽長はポケットへ手をつっ込んで拍手なんかどうでもいいというようにのそのそみんなの間を歩きまわっていましたが、じつはどうして嬉しさでいっぱいなのでした。みんなはたばこをくわえてマッチをすったり楽器をケースへ入れたりしました。

ホールはまだぱちぱち手が鳴っています。それどころではなくいよいよそれが高くなって何だかこわいような手がつけられないような音になりました。大きな白いリボンを胸につけた司会者がはいって来ました。

「アンコールをやっていますが、何かみじかいものでもきかせてやってくださいませんか。」

すると楽長がきっとなって答えました。

「いけませんな。こういう大物のあとへ何を出したってこっちの気の済むようには行くもんでないんです。」

「では楽長さん出て一寸挨拶してください。」

「だめだ。おい、ゴーシュ君、何か出て弾いてやってくれ。」

「わたしがですか。」ゴーシュは呆気にとられました。

「君だ、君だ。」ヴァイオリンの一番の人がいきなり顔をあげて云いました。

「さあ出て行きたまえ。」楽長が云いました。みんなもセロをむりにゴーシュに持たせて扉をあけるといきなり舞台へゴーシュを押し出してしまいました。ゴーシュがその孔のあい

had fallen silent and was listening intently. Gauche steadily played on. He finished the part where the cat had been in anguish and started giving off sparks, and he also finished the part where it had banged itself repeatedly against the door.

When the song finished, Gauche bolted backstage while holding his cello as quickly as that cat, without even glancing at the audience. And in the dressing room, he saw the conductor, and then his colleagues, sitting there staring silently as if they were looking at a fire. Gauche felt that he had nothing else to lose, so he quickly walked past his colleagues and sat down heavily on the couch that was on the other side of the room, crossing his legs.

Then, all of them turned to look at Gauche, but they didn't particularly look like they were laughing. They looked serious.

"Tonight is a strange night," Gauche thought.

But the conductor stood up and said, "Hey Gauche, that was great! Despite your song choice, everyone was listening seriously. You managed to prepare that kind of performance in about ten days. If you compare how you are now with how you were then, it would be like comparing a baby to a soldier! I guess you always could have done it if you had put your mind to it."

All of his colleagues also came and stood up, and congratulated Gauche.

"Well, it's because his body is so healthy that he was able to do it. If he was an ordinary person, he would have died," the conductor said from across the room.

Gauche returned home late that night.

たセロをもってじつに困ってしまって舞台へ出るとみんなはそら見ろというように一そうひどく手を叩きました。わあと叫んだものもあるようでした。
「どこまでひとをばかにするんだ。よし見ていろ。印度の虎狩をひいてやるから。」ゴーシュはすっかり落ちついて舞台のまん中へ出ました。
それからあの猫の来たときのようにまるで怒った象のような勢で虎狩りを弾きました。ところが聴衆はしいんとなって一生けん命聞いています。ゴーシュはどんどん弾きました。猫が切ながってぱちぱち火花を出したところも過ぎました。扉へからだを何べんもぶっつけた所も過ぎました。
曲が終るとゴーシュはもうみんなの方などは見もせずちょうどその猫のようにすばやくセロをもって楽屋へ遁げ込みました。すると楽屋では楽長はじめ仲間がみんな火事にでもあったあとのように眼をじっとしてひっそりとすわり込んでいます。ゴーシュはやぶれかぶれだと思ってみんなの間をさっさとあるいて行って向うの長椅子へどっかりとからだをおろして足を組んですわりました。
するとみんなが一ぺんに顔をこっちへ向けてゴーシュを見ましたがやはりまじめでべつにわらっているようでもありませんでした。
「こんやは変な晩だなあ。」
ゴーシュは思いました。ところが楽長は立って云いました。
「ゴーシュ君、よかったぞお。あんな曲だけれどもここではみんなかなり本気になって聞いてたぞ。一週間か十日の間にずいぶん仕上げたなあ。十日前とくらべたらまるで赤ん

Again he gulped down water. He opened the window and thought of the cuckoo who had flown away, gazing at the faraway sky.

"Oh, cuckoo. I'm sorry for what I did to you that time. It's not that I was angry," he said.

坊と兵隊だ。やろうと思えばいつでもやれたんじゃないか、君。」
仲間もみんな立って来て
「よかったぜ。」とゴーシュに云いました。
「いや、からだが丈夫だからこんなこともできるよ。普通の人なら死んでしまうからな。」楽長が向うで云っていました。
その晩遅くゴーシュは自分のうちへ帰って来ました。
そしてまた水をがぶがぶ呑みました。それから窓をあけていつかかっこうの飛んで行ったと思った遠くのそらをながめながら
「ああかっこう。あのときはすまなかったなあ。おれは怒ったんじゃなかったんだ。」と云いました。

*** [LESSON FOR PART ONE] ***

Translator's Notes

1. The protagonist's name, ゴーシュ **Gōshu**, can be considered to have originated from a French word *gauche*, which means "left" or "clumsy." On the other hand, Umezu (2005) argues that this name originates from a classic German word *Gauch*, which means "cuckoo."
2. 活動写真 **katsudō-shashin** was rendered as "moving picture" rather than "film" or "movie" in order to show the time frame of the original Japanese text.
3. ドレミファ **do-re-mi-fa** is "solfege," which is very commonly known in Japan. However, it was rendered as "scales" because it is more commonly known in North America.
4. **Miyazawa Kenji** is well-known for his extensive use of onomatopoeias. Some of his creative onomatopoeias were transliterated and retained, but most onomatopoeias were rendered as lexical words or as descriptions because onomatopoeias are not a standard feature of the English language, as in Japanese.

Vocabulary and Expressions

- セロ **sero** cello (It is more commonly called チェロ **chero** now.)
- セロ弾(ひ)き **sero-hiki** cellist
- 活動写真館(かつどうしゃしんかん) **katsudō-shashinkan** (silent) moving-picture theater
- 係(かか)り **kakari** person in charge
- あんまり **anmari** = あまり **amari**
- 評判(ひょうばん) **hyōban** reputation
- …どころではない ... **dokoro de wa nai** to be far more than ...
- 実(じつ)は **jitsu wa** in fact
- 仲間(なかま) **nakama** fellow, group-mate
- 楽手(がくしゅ) **gakushu** musicians
- 楽長(がくちょう) **gakuchō** conductor
- いじめる **ijimeru** to treat harshly
- ひるすぎ（昼過(ひるす)ぎ） **hirusugi** afternoon
- 楽屋(がくや) **gakuya** backstage, dressing room behind the stage

- 円(まる)く **maruku** in a circle
- ならぶ **narabu** to line up
- 音楽会(おんがくかい) **ongakukai** or **ongakkai** music concert
- 第六交響曲(だいろくこうきょうきょく) **dai-roku kōkyōkyoku** the *Sixth Symphony*
- トランペット **toranpetto** trumpet
- 歌(うた)う **utau** to sing
- ヴァイオリン **baiorin** violin
- 二(ふた)いろ **futairo** two colors
- …風(ふう) **... fū** ... style
- 鳴(な)る **naru** to sound
- クラリネット **kurarinetto** clarinet
- ボーボー **bō-bō** [MIMETIC] the sound of clarinet
- 手伝(てつだ)う **tetsudau** to help, support
- りんと **rin to** with a dignified look
- 口(くち)を結(むす)ぶ **kuchi o musubu** to purse one's lips
- 眼(め)を皿(さら)のようにする **me o sara no yō ni suru** to open one's eyes widely like saucers
- 楽譜(がくふ) **gakufu** sheet music, score
- 見(み)つめる **mitsumeru** to stare at
- …ながら **... nagara** while ...

  [GRAMMAR] ながら follows a verb in the stem form and expresses an accompanying activity.

  EXAMPLE:

  テレビを見(み)ながら晩(ばん)ご飯(はん)を食(た)べました。

  Terebi o minagara ban-gohan o tabemashita.

  I ate dinner while watching TV.
- 一心(いっしん)に **isshin ni** intently
- にわかに **niwaka ni** suddenly
- ぱたっ **patat** [MIMETIC] clapping hands
- 両手(りょうて) **ryōte** both hands
- ぴたり **pitari** [MIMETIC] suddenly
- 曲(きょく) **kyoku** song, piece of music
- やめる **yameru** to quit
- しん **shin** [MIMETIC] quiet
- どなる **donaru** to shout
- おくれる **okureru** to delay, to be late
- トォテテ　テテテイ **tōtete tetetei** [MIMETIC] melody line that they were playing
- やり直(な)す **yarinaosu** to redo
- はい **hai** Now!
- 顔(かお) **kao** face

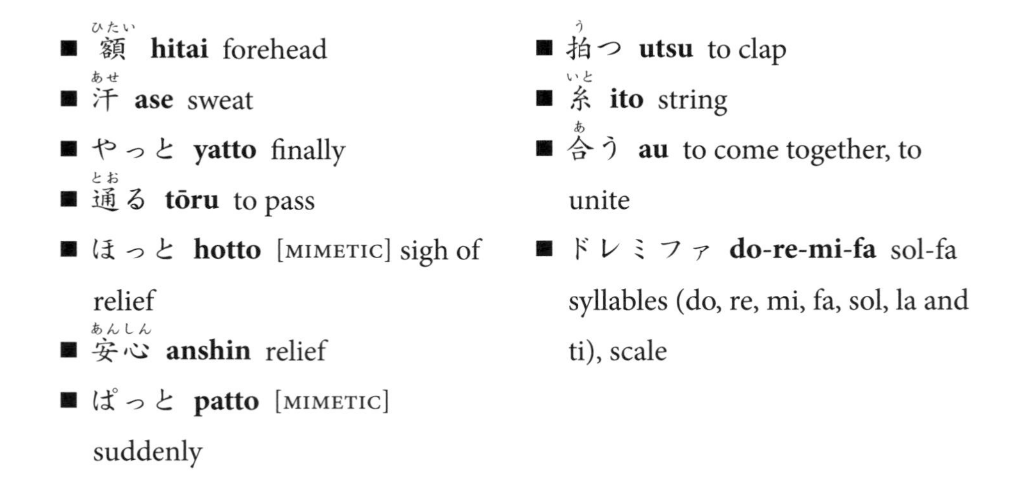

- 額(ひたい) **hitai** forehead
- 汗(あせ) **ase** sweat
- やっと **yatto** finally
- 通(とお)る **tōru** to pass
- ほっと **hotto** [MIMETIC] sigh of relief
- 安心(あんしん) **anshin** relief
- ぱっと **patto** [MIMETIC] suddenly
- 拍(う)つ **utsu** to clap
- 糸(いと) **ito** string
- 合(あ)う **au** to come together, to unite
- ドレミファ **do-re-mi-fa** sol-fa syllables (do, re, mi, fa, sol, la and ti), scale

Exercises

Select the most appropriate item in the parentheses.

1. ゴーシュはセロ弾(ひ)きですが、あまり上手(じょうず)でないと（いる・いう）評判(ひょうばん)でした。

2. ひるすぎに、楽屋(がくや)でみんなは音楽会(おんがっかい)に出(だ)す曲(きょく)の練習(れんしゅう)を（する・して）いました。

3. ゴーシュは目(め)を皿(さら)のようにして楽譜(がくふ)を見(み)つめ（たり・ながら）、一心(いっしん)に弾(ひ)きました。

4. 楽長(がくちょう)がぱたっと手をたたいて、みんな（ぴたり・ふわり）と曲(きょく)をやめてしんとしました。

5. 楽長(がくちょう)は「セロが（おくれた・わすれた）。」とどなり、みんなはやり直(なお)しをしました。

6. しばらく弾くと、楽長がまたぱっと手をたたいて、「セロ。（糸・曲）が合わない。」と言いました。

7. 楽長はゴーシュにドレミファを（教えて・教える）いるひまはないと言いました。

Discussion Questions

1. Find out more about Miyazawa Kenji's background, and share with your friends/classmates.

2. Do you think this story took place in Japan? Why or why not?

3. Do you play any musical instruments? Describe your experience.

✻✻✻ [LESSON FOR PART TWO] ✻✻✻

Translator's Notes

金星音楽団 **Kinsei ongakudan** is the name of the orchestra. It was rendered semantically although names are often transliterated in translated texts.

Vocabulary and Expressions

- ■ 気の毒な **kinodoku na** pitiful
- ■ …そうな **... sō na** appearing ...
  [GRAMMAR] そうな follows a verb or an adjective in the stem form and creates a new **na**-type adjective that means ...“-looking”.
  EXAMPLE:
  あの人はこわそうですね。
  Ano hito wa kowasō desu ne.
  That person looks scary.
- ■ わざと **waza to** on purpose
- ■ じぶん **jibun** self
- ■ 譜 **fu** = 楽譜 **gakufu** sheet music, music score
- ■ のぞき込む **nozokikomu** to peer at

■ 楽器 **gakki** (musical) instrument

■ はじく **hajiku** to flick

■ あわてて **awatete** hurriedly, hastily

■ 直す **naosu** to fix

■ ずいぶん **zuibun** quite

■ 小節 **shōsetsu** measure, (musical) bar

■ 口をまげる **kuchi o mageru** to twist one's mouth

■ 進む **susumu** to progress

■ あんばい **anbai** condition, state

■ おどす **odosu** to threaten

■ 形 **katachi** form, shape

■ どきっ **dokit** [MIMETIC] heartbeat

■ 別の **betsu no** other

■ 考える **kangaeru** to think over

■ ふり **furi** pretending

EXAMPLE:
熊が来たので死んでいるふりをしました。
Kuma ga kita node shindeiru furi o shimashita.
Because a bear came, I pretended to be dead.

■ そらと思って **sora to omotte** to pull himself together

■ いきなり **ikinari** suddenly

■ どんと **don to** [MIMETIC] bang

■ 足を踏む **ashi o fumu** to stamp one's foot

■ どなる **donaru** to shout

■ …出す **... dasu** to start to do ... abruptly

EXAMPLE:
妹は泣き出しました。
Imōto wa nakidashimashita.
My little sister burst into tears.

■ まるでなっていない **marude natteinai** not right at all

■ 心臓 **shinzō** heart

■ がさがさ **gasa-gasa** [MIMETIC] dry and rough

■ 諸君 **shokun** Everyone!

■ 演奏 **ensō** (music) performance

■ 音楽 **ongaku** music

■ 専門 **senmon** specialty

■ 金沓鍛冶 **kanagutsu kaji** blacksmith

■ 砂糖屋 **satōya** sugar shop

■ 丁稚 **decchi** apprentice

■ …なんか **... nanka** such a thing like

■ 寄り集まり **yori-atsumari** gathering

- ■ 負(ま)ける **makeru** to be defeated
- ■ われわれの **ware-ware no** our
- ■ 面目(めんもく) **menmoku** honor
- ■ おい **oi** interjection used for getting attention bluntly
- ■ 表情(ひょうじょう) **hyōjō** expressions
- ■ 怒(おこ)る **okoru** to get angry
- ■ 喜(よろこ)ぶ **yorokobu** to get delighted
- ■ 感情(かんじょう) **kanjō** emotion
- ■ さっぱり **sappari** (not) at all
- ■ 出(で)る **deru** to come out
- ■ ぴたっ **pitat** [MIMETIC] perfect togetherness
- ■ 外(そと)の **soto no** other
- ■ 合(あ)う **au** to match, to come together
- ■ 靴(くつ)のひも **kutsu no himo** shoelace
- ■ 引(ひ)きずる **hikizuri** to drag
- ■ ついてくる **tsuitekuru** to follow (us)

  EXAMPLE:

  犬(いぬ)がついてきました。

  Inu ga tsuite kimashita.

  A dog followed me.
- ■ 光輝(こうき)ある **kōkiaru** splendid
- ■ 金星(きんせい) **kinsei** Venus (planet)
- ■ …団(だん) **... dan** group, association

  EXAMPLES:

  医師団(いしだん) **ishi-dan** *team of doctors*, 暴力団(ぼうりょくだん) **bōryoku-dan** *gangster organization*
- ■ …のために **... no tame ni** for ...
- ■ 悪評(あくひょう) **akuhyō** bad reputation
- ■ かっきり **kakkiri** [MIMETIC] exactly, just (in terms of time)
- ■ ボックス **bokkusu** = オーケストラボックス **ōkesutora-bokkusu** orchestra pit
- ■ …てくれ給(たま)え **... te kuretamae** Please do ...
- ■ おじぎ **ojigi** bow
- ■ くわえる **kuwaeru** to hold in one's mouth
- ■ マッチ **matchi** match
- ■ する **suru** to strike (match)
- ■ 出(で)て行(い)く **deteiku** to go out
- ■ …たり **-tari** do ..., etc. [GRAMMAR] Verbs and adjectives in the たり **tari**-form can be created just by adding り after their た **ta**-form (plain past form). The たり **tari**-form can be used to list actions and states as examples. Make sure to end the sentence with the verb する **suru**.

EXAMPLE:

食(た)べたり飲(の)んだりしました。

Tabetari non-dari shimashita.

We ate, drink, etc.

- ■ …みたいな **... mitai a** -looking
  [GRAMMAR] みたいな can follow a noun to create a **na**-type adjective that means "-looking."

  EXAMPLE:

  クマみたいな犬(いぬ) **kuma mitai na inu** *a dog that looks like a bear*
- ■ 粗末(そまつ)な **somatsu na** shabby
- ■ 箱(はこ) **hako** box
- ■ かかえる **kakaeru** to hold or carry under or in the arms
- ■ 壁(かべ) **kabe** wall
- ■ 向(む)く **muku** to face
- ■ ぼろぼろ **boro-boro** [MIMETIC] falling (in drops)
- ■ 泪(なみだ) = 涙(なみだ) **namida** tears
- ■ こぼす **kobosu** to spill
- ■ 気(き)を取(と)り直(なお)す **ki o torinaosu** to pull oneself together

Exercises

Select the most appropriate item in the parentheses.

1. ゴーシュが怒(おこ)られたとき、みんなは気(き)の毒(どく)（よう・そう）にしました。

2. ゴーシュは（ゆっくり・あわてて）糸(いと)を直(なお)しました。

3. だいぶ進(すす)むと、また楽長(がくちょう)が（くっきり・ぱたっと）手(て)をうちました。

4. ゴーシュは（ぴたっと・どきっと）しましたが、怒(おこ)られたのは別(べつ)の人(ひと)でした。

5. また楽長(がくちょう)が足(あし)を（ぴたっと・どんと）踏(ふ)んで、ゴーシュをしかりました。

6. ゴーシュは感情(かんじょう)というものが（ある・ない）と言(い)われました。

7. それから、ゴーシュはいつもほかの楽器(がっき)（が・と）合(あ)わないと楽長(がくちょう)にしかられました。

8. 練習(れんしゅう)のあと、みんなはタバコをすったり、出(で)かけたり（ました・しました）。

9. ゴーシュは（壁(かべ)・てんじょう・まど）の方(ほう)を向(む)いて泣(な)きましたが、また一人(ひとり)で練習(れんしゅう)をはじめました。

Discussion Questions

1. Why did everyone look at their music or pluck their instruments "on purpose" when Gauche was scolded?

2. What kind of person do you think the conductor is? Why does he get angry so often?

3. How do you think Gauche felt after the rehearsal?

✻✻✻ [LESSON FOR PART THREE] ✻✻✻

Vocabulary and Expressions

- 巨(おお)きな = 大(おお)きな **ōkina** big
- しょう **shou** = 背負(せお)う **seou** to carry something on one's back
- 町(まち)はずれ **machi-hazure** outskirts (of a town)
- 川(かわ)ばた **kawabata** riverbank
- こわれる **kowareru** to break down
- 水車(すいしゃ) **suisha** water mill
- 小屋(こや) **koya** hut, shack
- たった **tatta** just
- 畑(はたけ) **hatake** vegetable plot

■ 枝 **eda** branch of a tree

■ 甘藍 キャベジ **kyabeji** (= キャベツ **kyabetsu**) cabbage

■ 虫 **mushi** bugs

■ ひろう **hirou** to pick up

■ 包み **tsutsumi** wrapped item (package)

■ ごつごつ **gotsu-gotsu** [MIMETIC] rugged

■ 夕方 **yūgata** dusk

■ そっと **sotto** [MIMETIC] quietly

■ 床 **yuka** floor

■ 置く **oku** to put something somewhere

EXAMPLE:

本をテーブルの上に置きました。

Hon o tēburu no ue ni okimashita.

I put my book on the table.

■ いきなり **ikinari** abruptly

■ 棚 **tana** shelf

■ コップ **koppu** glass, cup

■ バケツ **baketsu** bucket

■ 水 **mizu** water

■ ごくごく **goku-goku** [MIMETIC] gulping repetitively

■ ふる（振る）**furu** to shake

■ 虎 **tora** tiger

■ 勢 **ikioi** force, energy

■ めくる **mekuru** to turn (pages), to flip (sheets)

■ 考える **kagaeru** to think about, to brood

■ しまい **shimai** end

■ なんべんも（何遍も）**nanben mo** numerous times [GRAMMAR] 遍 **hen** is a counter for occasions. Its pronunciation changes depending on the preceding sound, as in 一遍 **ippen**, 二遍 **nihen** and 三遍 **sanben**. When a counter is used between a question word and the particle も **mo**, it expresses numerous quantity or a large amount.

EXAMPLE:

何遍もあやまりました。

Nanben mo ayamarimashita.

I apologized numerous times.

■ ごうごう **gō-gō** [MIMETIC] thunderous sound

■ とうに **tō ni** a long time ago

■ …しまう **... shimau** to have done ... [GRAMMAR] しまう can follow a verb in the **te**-form and shows that the action is completely done and irreversible, often indicating the speaker's regret.

EXAMPLE:

漢字を忘れてしまいました。

Kanji o wasurete shimaimashita.

I have forgotten kanji.

■ 血走る **chibashiru** to become bloodshot

■ 物凄い **monosugoi** terrible, frightful, horrible

■ 顔つき **kaotsuki** facial expression

■ いまにも **imanimo** at any moment

■ 倒れる **taoreru** to collapse

■ …ように見える **... yō ni mieru** to appear ...

■ 誰か **dareka** someone

■ 扉 **to** (= とびら **tobira**) door

■ とんとん **ton-ton** [MIMETIC] knocking

■ 叩く **tataku** to knock (on the door), to hit

■ ねぼける **nebokeru** to be half asleep

■ すうと **sūto** (= すうっと **sūtto**) [MIMETIC] smoothly without sound

■ 叫ぶ **sakebu** to shout

■ 三毛猫 **mike-neko** cat with three colors of fur (colors)

■ 押す **osu** to push

■ 半分 **hanbun** halfway

■ 熟す **jukusu** to ripen

■ さも **samo** just one glance tells you

■ 重そう **omosō** to appear heavy

■ …そうな **... sō na** ...-looking

[GRAMMAR] そうな follows a verb or an adjective in the stem form and creates a new **na**-type adjective that means "looks like ..."

EXAMPLES:

こわれそうな車 **kowaresō na kuruma** *a car that looks like it is going to break down*

幸せそうな人 **shiawasesō na hito** *a person who appears happy*

■ おろす **orosu** to put something down

■ くたびれる **kutabireru** to get tired

■ 運搬 **unpan** carrying things

■ おみや **omiya** = おみやげ **omiyage** souvenir

- むしゃくしゃ **mushakusha** [MIMETIC] irritation, stress
- どなりつける **donaritsukeru** to shout at
- きさま **kisama** the second person (derogatory) pronoun
- 食(く)う **ku'u** to eat (derogatory)
- むしる **mushiru** to pick
- 茎(くき) **kuki** stem (of plants)
- かじる **kajiru** to chew, to bite
- けちらす **kechirasu** to kick around
- …め **... me** a particle for derogatory emphasis
- 肩(かた) **kata** shoulder
- すぼめる **subomeru** to make something narrower
- にやにや **niya-niya** [MIMETIC] smirk
- からだにさわる **karada ni sawaru** to harm one's health
- シューマン **Shūman** Schumann
- トロメライ **Toromerai** *Träumerei*
- …ごらんなさい **... goran'nasai** = …みなさい **... minasai** try doing ...
- きいてあげる **ki'iteageru** to listen ... for you
- 生意気(なまいき)な **namaiki na** audacious, smart aleck
- …のくせに **... no kuse ni** in spite of ...
- しゃくにさわる **shaku ni sawaru** to irritate
- 遠慮(えんりょ) **enryo** reservation
- ねむられる **nemurareru** = ねむれる **nemureru** to be able to sleep [GRAMMAR] Verbs in the potential form such as 食(た)べられる **taberareru** and 飲(の)める **nomeru** express one's ability.

  EXAMPLE:

  漢字(かんじ)が読(よ)めますか。

  Kanji ga yome-masu ka.

  Can you read kanji?

Exercises

Select the most appropriate item in the parentheses.

1. ゴーシュは家へ帰ると、まず水を（ごうごう・ごくごく）のみました。

2. それから、（猫・虎）みたいな勢でいっしょうけんめいセロの練習をしました。

3. 夜中はとうに過ぎて（しまって・おわって）いました。

4. すると、猫がトマトを（重く・重そうに）もって入って来ました。

5. 猫はゴーシュに「シューマンのトロメライを弾いてごらんなさい。聞いて（もらう・あげる）から。」といいました。

6. ゴーシュは猫が生意気だと思って、（おこり・つかれ）ました。

7. 猫はゴーシュの音楽をきかないと、（ねない・ねられない）といいました。

Discussion Questions

1. What do you think of the environment of Gauche's home?

2. How do you think Gauche felt when he started practicing his cello at home?

3. What did the cat do that made Gauche upset?

⁂ [LESSON FOR PART FOUR] ⁂

Translator's Notes

足ぶみ **ashibumi** can be rendered either as "to stamp" or "to stomp" depending on the context. However, if it is only one pressing step, "to stamp" seems to be the better choice.

Vocabulary and Expressions

- 足ぶみ **ashibumi** stamping
- にわかに **niwaka ni** suddenly
- かぎをかう（鍵をかう）**kagi o kau** to lock
- あかし **akashi** = あかり **akari** light
- 消す **kesu** to put out, to turn off
- 二十日過ぎ **hatsuka sugi** after the twentieth day (phase of the moon)
- ひかり **hikari** light
- 室 = 部屋 **heya** room
- 澄ます **sumasu** to assume a composed look
- 作曲 **sakkyoku** composing
- はんけち **hankechi** = ハンカチ **hankachi** handkerchief
- 引きさく **hikisaku** to tear up
- 穴 **ana** hole
- ぎっしり **gisshiri** [MIMETIC] tightly
- つめる（詰める）**tsumeru** to stuff into
- 嵐 **arashi** storm
- 印度 = インド **Indo** India
- 虎狩り **toragari** tiger hunt
- …はじめる **... hajimeru** to start -ing [GRAMMAR] はじめる is a verb that means "to start," but it can follow a verb in the stem form to mean "to start -ing."

  EXAMPLE:

  五時に勉強をしはじめました。

  Go-ji ni benkyō o shihajimemashita.

  I started to study at 5 p.m.
- 首 **kubi** neck
- 曲げる **mageru** to tilt

- パチパチパチ **pachi-pachi-pachi** [MIMETIC] sparks
- ぱっと **patto** [MIMETIC] rapidly
- 飛びのく **tobinoku** to jump out
- 一生一代 **issei-ichidai** once in a lifetime
- 失敗 **shippai** failure
- …という風に **... to iu fū ni** like ...
- あわてる **awateru** to panic
- 額 **hitai** forehead
- 火花 **hibana** spark
- ひげ **hige** whiskers
- くすぐったい **kusuguttai** ticklish
- くしゃみ **kushami** sneeze
- 顔 **kao** face
- こうしてはいられない **kōshite wa irarenai** cannot stay like this
- はせあるく **hase-aruku** to trot
- ますます **masu-masu** increasingly
- 勢よく **ikioi-yoku** vigorously
- ご生ですから **goshō desu kara** I am begging you
- タクト **takuto** baton
- だまれ **damare** shut up
- つかまえる（捕まえる）**tsukamaeru** to catch
- くるしがる **kurushigaru** to appear to be suffering
- はねあがる **haneagaru** to jump up
- 壁 **kabe** wall
- くっつける **kuttsukeru** to let something touch something else
- ぐるぐる **guru-guru** [MIMETIC] rolling or turning
- 風車 **fūsha** windmill
- 許す **yurusu** to forgive
- ようよう **yōyō** finally
- やめる **yameru** to quit
- けろりと **kerori to** [MIMETIC] completely, entirely
- けろりとする **kerori to suru** to completely go back to normal
- 演奏 **ensō** performance
- …はどうかしている **... wa dō ka shiteiru** Something is wrong with ...
- ぐっと **gutto** [MIMETIC] considerably
- しゃくにさわる **shaku ni sawaru** to irritate

- ■ 何気なく **nanigenaku** unintentionally
- ■ …風で **... fū de** in a way ...
- ■ 巻たばこ **maki-tabaco** cigar
- ■ 工合 = 具合 **guai** physical condition
- ■ 舌 **shita** tongue
- ■ ばかにする **baka ni suru** to make a fool of
- ■ 尖った **togatta** pointy
- ■ ベロリ **berori** [MIMETIC] licking or movement of a tongue
- ■ 荒れる **areru** rough
- ■ シュッと **shutto** [MIMETIC] swishing
- ■ 愕く = 驚く **odoroku** to be astonished
- ■ よろよろ **yoro-yoro** [MIMETIC] tottering
- ■ にげみち **nigemichi** escape path
- ■ こさえる **kosaeru** to make
- ■ …ようとする **... yō to suru** to try to do ... [GRAMMAR] A verb in the volitional form followed by とする expresses an attempt.

  EXAMPLE:

  寝ようとしましたが寝られませんでした。

  Neyō to shimashita ga nerare-masen deshita.

  I tried to sleep, but I couldn't.
- ■ ばか **baka** idiot
- ■ 萱 **kaya** miscanthus reed
- ■ せいせいする **sei-sei suru** to feel refreshed
- ■ ぐっすり **gussuri** [MIMETIC] sleeping deeply
- ■ ねむる（眠る）**nemuru** to sleep

Exercises

Select the most appropriate item in the parentheses.

1. ゴーシュは楽長の（しました・した）ように足ぶみをしてどなりました。

2. しかし、急に気を変え、扉や窓をしめて、『印度の虎狩り』という曲を（弾く・弾き）はじめました。

3. そうすると、三毛猫は眼を（パチパチ・ペロリ）として、眼や額やひげから火花を出しました。

4. それから、壁にからだをくっつけて、そのあとは（青く・青い）ひかり、ぐるぐるまわりました。

5. 三毛猫はもうゴーシュの（タクト・セロ）をとるようなことはしないから、やめてくれといいました。

6. ゴーシュもぐるぐるして来たのでやめると、三毛猫がまた（かわいい・生意気な）ことをいいました。

7. ゴーシュはしゃくにさわりましたが、「どうだい。ぐあいを悪くしないかい。舌をだしてごらん。」といって、三毛猫に（手・舌）を出させると、マッチですりました。

8. 三毛猫はゴーシュのまわりを風車の（こと・よう）にぐるぐるまわりました。

9. そして、よろよろにげみちをこさえようと（なり・し）ました。

10. ゴーシュはしばらくしたら、三毛猫をへやから出して（やり・もらい）ました。

Discussion Questions

1. Listen to *Träumerei* composed by Schumann on the Internet. What kind of music do you think it is?

2. Why do you think Gauche closed the door and the windows?

3. Do you think Gauche played "Tiger Hunting in India" well? Why?

4. How do you think Gauche felt after the cat left?

⁂ [LESSON FOR PART FIVE] ⁂

Translator's Notes

Excessive repetition of the onomatopoeia かっこう **kakkō** in this context is stylistically marked in Japanese, so it is preserved in the English translation. The repetition in this context has an auditory effect that is essential for describing and making the bird's determination felt.

Vocabulary and Expressions

- そっくり **sokkuri** completely, entirely
- ぐんぐん **gun-gun** [MIMETIC] progress
- 間(ま)もなく **mamonaku** soon
- 過(す)ぎる **sugiru** to pass
- 屋根裏(やねうら) **yaneura** attic
- こっこっ **kokkok** [MIMETIC] knocking
- こりる **koriru** to learn the hard way
- 叫(さけ)ぶ **sakebu** to shout
- 天井(てんじょう) **tenjō** ceiling
- ぽろん **poron** [MIMETIC] light popping sound
- 一疋(いっぴき) = 一匹(いっぴき) **ippiki** one (counter for animals)
- 灰(はい)いろ **hai-iro** gray
- 鳥(とり) **tori** bird
- とまる **tomaru** to be docked
- かっこう **kakkō** cuckoo
- …まで **... made** even ...
- 用(よう) **yō** task
- 教(おそ)わる **osowaru** to learn, to be taught
- 啼(な)く **naku** to sing (bird)
- なきよう **nakiyō** = なきかた **nakikata** the way of singing/crying (bird)

- なかま **nakama** group member (member of the same category)
- ... なら **... nara** if ..., if you are talking about ...
- 勝手 **katte** your choice
- 正確に **seikaku ni** precisely, accurately
- くそ **kuso** shit
- 外国 **gaikoku** foreign country
- つく **tsuku** to accompany
- うるさい **urusai** annoying
- さっさと **sassato** [MIMETIC] quickly
- ボロンボロン **boron-boron** [MIMETIC] plucking strings
- 羽 **hane** wing
- ばたばた **batabata** [MIMETIC] flapping
- しばらく **shibaraku** for a while
- 構える **kamaeru** to take a fighting stance
- 第六交響楽 **dai-roku kōkyō-gaku** the *Sixth Symphony*
- 続ける **tsuzukeru** to continue
- よろこぶ（喜ぶ）**yorokobu** to be delighted
- いつまでも **itsumade mo** forever, indefinitely
- とうとう **tōtō** finally
- 痛い **itai** painful
- …なる **... naru** to become ...

  [GRAMMAR] The verb なる can follow an adverb to express some change in some state and means "to become ..." or "to start ..."

  EXAMPLE:

  歌がうまくなりました。

  Uta ga umaku narimashita.

  I became skillful in singing.
- いいかげんにしないか **iikagen ni shinai ka** That's enough.
- …ながら **... nagara** while ...

  [GRAMMAR] ながら can follow a verb in the stem form and expresses an accompanying activity.

  EXAMPLE:

  兄はギターを弾きながら歌います。

  Ani wa gitā o hikinagara utaimasu.

  My big brother sings as he plays the guitar.
- 残念な **zan'nen** disappointed
- つりあげる **tsuriageru** to raise
- やめる **yameru** to quit

Exercises

Select the most appropriate item in the parentheses.

1. ゴーシュがセロの練習をして（いた・いる）と、屋根裏をこつこつ叩く音が聞こえました。

2. ゴーシュがこたえると、天井（を・から）かっこうが降りてきました。

3. かっこうはドレミファをゴーシュに正確に（教え・教わり）たいといいました。

4. ゴーシュがボロンボロンと糸を合わせてドレミファソラシドと弾くと、かっこうは（そうです・ちがいます）といって「かっこう」となきました。

5. そのあとゴーシュが「かっこうかっこうかっこう」とセロでつづけて弾くと、かっこうも「かっこうかっこうかっこう」とつづけて（なきました・弾きました）。

6. ゴーシュはとうとう手が（痛い・痛く）なりました。それで、「こら。いいかげんにしないか。」と（いう・いい）ながらやめました。

Discussion Questions

1. Have you ever heard cuckoos sing? How did you feel?

2. Have you practiced the scales while singing or playing string instruments? How did you do it? How was the experience?

[LESSON FOR PART SIX]

Translator's Notes

The cuckoo's signing was rendered as "singing" or "crying" depending on the context. When the cuckoo's focus is on music, "singing" is used. When it is on the intensity and dedication, "crying" is used.

Vocabulary and Expressions

- すっかり **sukkari** completely
- 済む **sumu** to be completed
- …ようだ **... yō da** It appears that ... [GRAMMAR] ようだ can express one's conjecture by being placed at the end of a sentence. The predicate placed before ようだ must be in the prenominal form.

  EXAMPLE:
  今、日本円は高いようですね。
  Ima, Nihon-en wa takaiyō desu ne.
  It appears that Japanese yen is expensive now.
- こんこん **kon-kon** [MIMETIC] sharp movement
- 弓 **yumi** bow (of an instrument)
- 息 **iki** breath
- 永く＝長く **nagaku** long (time)
- にが笑い **niga-warai** bitter smile, forced smile
- 本気 **honki** seriousness
- はまっている **hamatteiru** to fit
- …という気がする **... to iu ki ga suru** to feel like ...
- 弾けば弾くほど… **hikeba hiku hodo ...** the more (he) played, the more ...
- どしん **doshin** [MIMETIC] dull sound
- ふらふら **fura-fura** [MIMETIC] unsteady, dizzy
- 恨めしい **urameshī** to resent
- 恨めしそうに **urameshisō ni** looking resentfully
- 意気地ない **ikujinai** timid
- やつ **yatsu** person (derogatory)
- のど（喉） **nodo** throat
- 叫ぶ **sakebu** to shout
- まね **mane** behavior, action

- 指(さ)す **sasu** to point at
- 東(ひがし) **higashi** east
- ぼうっと **bōtto** [MIMETIC] faintly
- 銀(ぎん) **gin** silver
- 北(きた) **kita** north
- どんどん **doshin** steadily
- 黙(だま)れ **damare** Shut up!
- いい気(き)になる **iiki ni naru** to be full of oneself
- 出(で)て行(い)かんと **dete ikan to** = 出て行かないと **dete ikanai to** if you don't go out
- むしる **mushiru** to pluck
- 朝飯(あさめし) **asameshi** breakfast
- 踏(ふ)む **fumu** to step on ...
- びっくりする **bikkuri suru** to be surprised
- いきなり **ikinari** suddenly
- めがける **megakeru** to aim at
- 飛(と)び立(た)つ **tobitatsu** to take off, to fly away
- 硝子(がらす)（ガラス） **garasu** glass
- はげしく（激(はげ)しく） **hageshiku** strongly
- ぶっつける **buttsukeru** = ぶつける **butsukeru** to hit
- ばたっと **batatto** [MIMETIC] thump
- 落(お)ちる **ochiru** to fall down
- あわてる（慌(あわ)てる） **awateru** to hurry
- 元来(がんらい) **ganrai** originally
- するする **suru-suru** [MIMETIC] smoothly
- わく（枠(わく)） **waku** frame
- しきりに **shikiri ni** repeatedly
- がたがた **gata-gata** [MIMETIC] rattling
- ばっと **batto** [MIMETIC] bang
- 嘴(くちばし) **kuchibashi** beak
- つけね（付(つ)け根(ね)） **tsukene** base
- 血(ち) **chi** blood
- 待(ま)つ **matsu** to wait
- …寸 **-sun** an archaic measurement unit in Japan, approx. 1.193 inches
- 何(なに)が何(なん)でも **nani ga nan de mo** by all means, at all costs
- じっと **jitto** [MIMETIC] fixedly
- 向(むこ)う = 向(む)こう **mukō** opposite side
- みつめる **mitsumeru** to gaze

- ■ あらん限りの **aran kagiri no** all that one has
- ■ 力をこめる **chikara o komeru** to use all strength
- ■ ぱっと **patto** [MIMETIC] in a flash
- ■ もちろん **mochiron** of course
- ■ つきあたる（突き当たる） **tsukiataru** to crash into
- ■ …まま **... mama** while keeping ... [GRAMMAR] まま follows a verb in the た **ta**-form, an adjective in the pre-nominal form, a noun followed by の or a demonstrative adjective, and expresses a situation where the same state is maintained.

  EXAMPLE:

  立ったまま食べた。

  Tattamama tabeta.

  I ate standing.
- ■ 身動き **miugoki** moving of body
- ■ 飛ばす **tobasu** = とばせる **tobaseru** to make ... fly (the causative form of 飛ぶ **tobu**)
- ■ 飛びのく **tobinoku** to jump/fly out of the way
- ■ 飛びつく **tobitsuku** to jump at
- ■ 思わず **omowazu** reflexively, unintentionally
- ■ ける **keru** to kick
- ■ 物すごい **monosugoi** earth-shattering
- ■ 砕ける **kudakeru** to break into pieces
- ■ がらん **garan** [MIMETIC] emptiness
- ■ 矢 **ya** arrow
- ■ …のように **... no yō ni** just like ...

  EXAMPLE:

  魚のように泳ぎました。

  Sakana no yo ni oyogimashita.

  (He) swim like a fish.
- ■ 呆れる **akireru** to be taken aback
- ■ 倒れる **taoreru** to fall, to collapse
- ■ すみ（隅） **sumi** corner
- ■ ころがる（転がる） **korogaru** to fall over

Exercises

Select the most appropriate item in the parentheses.

1. 鳥はゴーシュの「かっこう」はいい（よう・そう）だけれども、何かちょっと違うと言いました。

2. つづけているうちに、ゴーシュも（鳥・自分）の方がドレミにはまっている気がしました。

3. そのとき、ゴーシュは（ゆっくり・いきなり）弾くのをやめました。

4. すると、鳥は（じっと・どしんと）頭をたたかれたようにふらふらしました。

5. 夜があけそうになって、鳥がもう一度ゴーシュに弾いてくれと頼むと、ゴーシュはどんと（天井・床）をふんで、「黙れっ。いい気になって。このばか鳥め。出て行かんとむしって朝飯に食ってしまうぞ。」とどなりました。

6. すると、鳥はびっくりして飛び立ち、ガラスに頭を（くっつけ・ぶつけ）て落ちました。

7. ゴーシュが窓を（あけよう・あける）としましたが、あきませんでした。

8. しかし、鳥はまたガラスにぶつかって落ち、見ると（目・くちばし）のところから血が出ていました。

9. ゴーシュが窓を開けようとしていると、また鳥がぶつかって、（落ちる・落ちた）まま身動きもしませんでした。

10. ゴーシュがつかまえて出してやろうとすると、また鳥が飛んだので、ゴーシュは窓を（たたいて・けって）ガラスをこわしました。

Discussion Questions

1. What did Gauche notice as he played the cello along with the bird's singing?

2. How does the author describe the scene where the bird hit the glass many times while Gauche struggled to help it? How did it make you feel?

3. How do you think Gauche felt after the bird left?

✻✻✻ [LESSON FOR PART SEVEN] ✻✻✻

Translator's Notes

子 **ko** means "child," but 狸の子 **tanuki no ko** was rendered as "baby raccoon" because the word "child" can only be used for humans in English. An alternative is "raccoon cub," but "baby raccoon" sounds more accessible for the target readers of this story.

Vocabulary and Expressions

■ つかれる（疲れる）**tsukareru** to get tired

■ こつこつ **kotsu-kotsu** [MIMETIC] knocking

■ 何が来ても **nani ga kite mo** no matter what comes [GRAMMAR] Question words in a phrase that ends in the **te**-form followed by も create a concessive clause that means "no matter ..."

- EXAMPLE:
  誰が何と言っても決心はかわりません。
  Dare ga nan to itte mo kesshin wa kawarimasen.
  No matter who says what, my decision will not change.
- おどかす **odokasu** to threaten
- 追い払う **oiharau** to chase out
- 待ち構える **machi-kamaeru** to be on the watch for
- 狸 **tanuki** raccoon
- …汁 **-jiru** soup with ...
- ぼんやり **bonyari** [MIMETIC] absentmindedly, faintly
- きちんと **kichinto** [MIMETIC] properly
- 吹き出す **fukidasu** to burst into laughter
- 無理に **muri ni** against one's desire
- キャベジ **kyabeji** = キャベツ **kyabetsu** cabbage
- 塩 **shio** salt
- まぜる **mazeru** to mix
- くたくた **kuta-kuta** [MIMETIC] cooking sound
- 煮る **niru** to cook
- ふしぎそうに（不思議そうに）**fushigisō ni** appearing confused
- 睡い＝眠い **nemui** sleepy
- 小太鼓 **kodaiko** small drum
- 合わせる **awaseru** to match (rhythm, speed, etc.)
- 棒きれ **bōkire** sticks
- 愉快な **yukai na** fun
- 馬車 **basha** carriage
- …屋 **-ya** ... shop
- ジャズ **jazu** jazz
- 変な **hen na** weird
- ちらちら **chira-chira** [MIMETIC] glancing
- 駒 **koma** bridge of a violin, cello, etc.
- 拍子 **hyōshi** tempo
- ぽんぽん **pon-pon** [MIMETIC] tapping
- なかなか **naka-naka** quite
- おしまい **oshimai** end
- 首 **kubi** neck
- 考える **kangaeru** to consider, to ponder
- 考えつく **kangaetsuku** to come up to (an idea or insight)

- きたい（期待） **kitai** expectation
- つまずく **tsumazuku** to stumble, to trip
- はっと **hatto** [MIMETIC] shock
- たしかに（確かに） **tashika ni** surely
- 手早く **tebayaku** quickly
- ゆうべ **yūbe** last night
- …気がする **... ki ga suru** to feel like ...
- 悪い **warui** bad
- 気の毒そうにする **kinodokusō ni suru** to be sympathetic
- …ながら **... nagara** while ...
- ゴムテープ **gomutēpu** elastic band
- ぱちん **pachin** [MIMETIC] snap
- とめる（留める） **tomeru** to keep in position
- 急いで **isoi de** hurriedly
- ぼんやりする **bonyari suru** [MIMETIC] to be absentminded
- 風 **kaze** wind
- 吸う **sū** to inhale
- とり戻す **torimodosu** to regain
- ねどこ（寝床） **nedoko** bed
- もぐり込む **mogurikomu** to dive under

Exercises

Select the most appropriate item in the parentheses.

1. またドアをノックする音がきこえましたが、ゴーシュは何が（来た・来て）もおどかして追い払おうと思いました。

2. それは狸の子でしたが、ゴーシュは狸の子に（狸汁・狸山）を知っているかとききました。

3. 狸の子はきちんと（座る・座った）まま「狸汁ってぼくしらない。」といいました。

4. ゴーシュは吹(ふ)き出(だ)しそうになりましたが、がまんしてこわい顔(かお)をして狸汁(たぬきじる)は狸(たぬき)を煮(に)てつくった（スープ・ごはん）だといいました。

5. 狸(たぬき)の子(こ)は父親(ちちおや)にゴーシュはいい人(ひと)だからゴーシュに小太鼓(こだいこ)を合(あ)わせて（もらう・あげる）ようにいわれたといいました。

6. 狸(たぬき)の子(こ)は棒(ぼう)でセロの駒(こま)の下(した)のところを拍子(ひょうし)を（もって・とって）叩(たた)きました。

7. 狸(たぬき)の子(こ)はゴーシュが二番目(にばんめ)の糸(いと)を弾(ひ)くときはきたい（で・に）遅(おく)れ、つまづくようになるといいました。

8. ゴーシュは「そうかもしれない。このセロは悪(わる)いんだよ。」（と・で）いいました。

9. 狸(たぬき)の子(こ)はゴーシュにもう一度(いちど)弾(ひ)いてくれといってゴーシュは明(あ)け方(がた)（まで・から）セロを弾(ひ)きました。

Discussion Questions

1. Why did Gauche almost burst out laughing?

2. Did Gauche find a problem as he played with the baby raccoon? Did he find a solution for it? Did he do something after that?

✻✻✻ [LESSON FOR PART EIGHT] ✻✻✻

Translator's Notes

1. 青(あお)い **aoi** in Japanese means "blue" or "green" depending on the context, although Japanese people can distinguish between these two colors.
2. There is no clue about the gender of the baby mouse in the original Japanese text. However, we took the liberty of using the masculine pronoun to refer to this baby mouse because using the pronoun "it" cannot express the closeness between the mother mouse and her baby.

Vocabulary and Expressions

- 夜通(よどお)し **yodōshi** throughout the night
- 明方(あけがた) **akegata** dawn
- 楽譜(がくふ) **gakufu** sheet music
- うとうと **uto-uto** [MIMETIC] dozing
- 聞(き)こえる **kikoeru** to be able to hear
- 位(くらい) **kurai** degree
- 野(の)ねずみ **no-nezumi** field mouse
- つれる **tsureru** to bring someone
- ちょろちょろ **choro-choro** [MIMETIC] daring about
- けしごむ **keshigomu** eraser
- …しか **... shika** only
- わらわれる（笑(わら)われる） **wara-wareru** to be laughed at
- きょろきょろ **kyoro-kyoro** [MIMETIC] looking around restlessly
- 青(あお)い **aoi** blue
- 栗(くり) **kuri** chestnut
- 実(み) **mi** nut, fruit
- …つぶ（粒(つぶ)） **... tsubu** a counter for grain or tiny pieces
- 児(こ)＝子(こ) **ko** child
- あんばい **anbai** health
- 慈悲(じひ) **jihi** mercy
- なおす（治(なお)す） **naosu** to cure
- 医者(いしゃ) **isha** medical doctor
- むっと **mutto** [MIMETIC] upset
- だまる **damaru** to be silent
- 思(おも)い切(き)る **omoi-kiru** to make up one's mind
- うそ **uso** lie

■ …のおかげで **... no okage de** thanks to ...

■ 兎 **usagi** rabbit

■ 意地悪 **ijiwaru** mean, nasty

■ みみずく **mimizuku** eared owl

■ お助け **o-tasuke** help (honorific)

■ 情 **jō** feeling

■ 楽隊 **gakutai** band

■ まね **mane** imitation, mimicry

■ 泣く **naku** to cry

■ …なら **... nara** if ... [GRAMMAR] Clauses with なら express the presupposition for your statement or question.

EXAMPLE:

日本で働きたいなら、日本語を勉強した方がいいですよ。

Nihon de hatarakitai nara, Nihon-go o benkyō-shita hō ga ii desu yo.

If you want to work in Japan, it is better to study Japanese.

■ …ば **-ba** if ... [GRAMMAR] Clauses with verbs and adjectives in the **ba**-form express a condition.

EXAMPLE:

これを飲めば、すっきりしますよ。

Kore o nomeba, sukkiri shimasu yo.

If you drink this, you'll feel refreshed.

■ …ればよかった **-reba yokatta** It should have been the case that ...

EXAMPLE:

私の言うことを聞けばよかったんです。

Watashi no iukoto o kikeba yokattan desu.

You should have listened to what I said.

■ さっき **sakki** a little while ago

■ 音 **oto** sound

■ いくら ... ても **ikura ... temo** no matter how ...

■ ふしあわせな（不幸せな） **fushiawase na** unhappy, misfortune

■ …や **... ya** ..., etc.

■ 片手 **katate** one hand

■ こする（擦る） **kosuru** to rub, to scrub

■ 床下 **yukashita** under the floor

■ 療す＝治す **naosu** to cure

■ 療る＝治る **naoru** to be cured [GRAMMAR] There are hundreds of transitive-intransitive verb pairs in Japanese. For example, 治す (to cure some illness) is a transitive verb and 治る (to be cured) is an intransitive verb.

EXAMPLES:

パソコンをこわしました。

Pasokon o kowashimashita.

I broke my computer.

パソコンがこわれました。

Pasokon ga kowaremashita.

My computer broke down.

- 血のまわり **chi no mawari** blood circulation
- あんまり **anmari** particularly
- 代わり **kawari** instead of
- ギウギウ **giu-giu** [MIMETIC] tightening strings
- くぐす **kugusu** to let something go through
- 顔 **kao** face
- 半分 **hanbun** half

Exercises

Select the most appropriate item in the parentheses.

1. ゴーシュは次の晩も夜通しセロを弾き、明方に楽譜を（もった・もって）ままうとうとしはじめました。

2. すると、ドアをノックする音がして、野ねずみが（青い・きいろい）栗をもってこどものねずみといっしょに入って来ました。

3. そのこどものねずみはとても（おおきくて・小さくて）、病気です。

4. 母ねずみはゴーシュにこどもの病気を（なおして・なおって）ほしいといいました。

5. ゴーシュは医者などできないと（むっと・うとうと）していいました。

6. 母ねずみは子ねずみはどうせ病気になるなら、もっと早く（なれば・なって）よかったといって泣き出しました。

7. 母ねずみによると、このあたりのものは病気になるとゴーシュのうちの（床下・天井）でゴーシュのセロの音をきいて病気をなおすそうです。

8. ゴーシュはやってみることにして、野ねずみのこどもをつまんでセロの孔（に・から）セロの中に入れてやりました。

9. おかあさんの野ねずみも中に入りたいというので、孔に入れてあげようとしましたが、（顔・手・足）が半分しかはいりませんでした。

Discussion Questions

1. Have you ever heard that music is good for our body and brain? Please share what you heard before or what you found through research on the Internet.

2. How do you think Gauche felt when he heard what the mother mouse said about the effect of his cello performance?

3. Who took care of you or took you to the hospital when you were sick during your childhood? What kind of things did he/she do for you? Talk about your memories.

✻✻✻ [LESSON FOR PART NINE] ✻✻✻

Translator's Notes

1. The repetition of ぶるぶる **buru-buru** used for the baby mouse's shivering is quite extensive and stylistically marked. This markedness was retained by adding the verb "to keep" and using two verbs, "trembling" and "shivering," in the English translation.

2. 腹の悪い **hara no warui** does not refer to any specific illness in this context. So, it was rendered as "sick" rather than using the word "stomach."

Vocabulary and Expressions

- ■ ばたばた **bata-bata** [MIMETIC] flapping or disturbance
- ■ そろえる **soroeru** to put in order
- ■ 蚊(か) **ka** mosquito
- ■ 声(こえ) **koe** voice
- ■ 底(そこ) **soko** bottom
- ■ 返事(へんじ)をする **henji o suru** to respond
- ■ 泣(な)き声(ごえ) **naki goe** crying voice
- ■ ラプソディー **rapusodī** rhapsody
- ■ 心配(しんぱい)そうに **shinpaisō ni** with a worried look
- ■ こらえる **koraeru** to endure
- ■ 目(め)をつぶる **me o tsuburu** to close one's eyes
- ■ ぶるぶる **buru-buru** [MIMETIC] shivering
- ■ ふるえる（震(ふる)える） **furueru** to shiver
- ■ 気分(きぶん) **kibun** feeling, mood
- ■ 起(お)き上(あ)がる **okiagaru** to rise, to get up
- ■ 走(はし)る **hashiru** to run
- ■ しきりに **shikiri ni** repeatedly
- ■ 何(なに)がな **nani gana** somehow, somewhat
- ■ かあいそう **ka'aisō** = かわいそう **kawaisō** How pitiful!
- ■ パン **pan** bread
- ■ きょろきょろ **kyoro-kyoro** [MIMETIC] looking around restlessly
- ■ 小麦(こむぎ) **komugi** wheat
- ■ 粉(こな) **kona** flour
- ■ こねる **koneru** to knead
- ■ むす **musu** to steam

■ ふくふく **fuku-fuku** [MIMETIC] puffiness
■ 膨らむ **fukuramu** to expand
■ おいしい **oishii** delicious
■ 戸棚 **todana** cupboard
■ お世話になる **o-sewa ni naru** to be taken care of
■ 運ぶ **hakobu** to carry
■ 一つまみ **hito-tsumami** one pinch
■ 置く **oku** to place something somewhere

EXAMPLE:
本をテーブルの上に置きました。
Hon o tēburu no ue ni okimashita.
I put the book on the table.

■ むしる **mushiru** to pluck, to tear, to pick
■ 大事な **daijina** precious
■ どっかり **dokkari** [MIMETIC] collapsing
■ 倒れる **taoreru** to collapse
■ ぐうぐう **gū-gū** [MIMETIC] deep sleep or snoring

Exercises

Select the most appropriate item in the parentheses.

1. 野ねずみはこどもに落ちるときにいつも教えている（よう・そう）に足をそろえてうまく落ちたかききました。

2. すると、こどものねずみは「いい。うまく落ちた。」と、まるで（猫・蚊・鳥）のような声でいいました。

3. こどものねずみをセロの中に（入れる・入れた）まま、ゴーシュはセロを弾きました。

4. 野ねずみのおかあさんは心配そうにきいていましたが、とうとうこらえ（きれない・きれなく）なって、もうこどもを出してやってくれといいました。

5. ゴーシュは孔(あな)のところに手(て)をあてて、ねずみのこどもを出(だ)して（やり・もらい）ました。

6. ねずみのこどもはしばらく（きょろきょろ・ぶるぶる）ふるえていました。

7. しかし、少(すこ)しすると、よくなって（走(はし)って・走(はし)る・走(はし)り）だしました。

8. ゴーシュは野(の)ねずみにパンを（一(ひと)つまみ・一(ひと)つぶ）あげました。

Discussion Questions

1. What do you think of the relationship between the mother mouse and the baby mouse?

2. Why do you think Gauche gave a piece of bread to the mice?

3. The baby mouse went inside the cello through a hole. What kind of hole do you think it was?

＊＊＊ [LESSON FOR PART TEN] ＊＊＊

Vocabulary and Expressions

- 公会堂(こうかいどう) **kōkaidō** town hall
- ホール **hōru** hall
- 裏(うら) **ura** back side
- 控室(ひかえしつ) **hikaeshitsu** backstage
- ほてらす **hoterasu** to make ... flush
- ぞろぞろ **zoro-zoro** [MIMETIC] in succession
- 引(ひ)きあげる **hiki-ageru** to return

  EXAMPLE:
  戦争(せんそう)が終(お)わって兵士(へいし)が自分(じぶん)の国(くに)に引(ひ)き上(あ)げて来(き)た。

Sensō ga owatte heishi ga jibun no kuni ni hikiagetekita.
The war ended and the soldiers came back to their homeland.

- めいめい **mei-mei** each
- 舞台 **butai** stage
- 首尾よく **shubi-yoku** successfully
- 拍手 **hakushu** applause, clapping
- ポケット **poketto** pocket
- のそのそ **noso-noso** [MIMETIC] sluggishly, slowly
- 嬉しさ **ureshisa** happiness, joy
- いっぱい **ippai** full
- ぱちぱち **pachi-pachi** [MIMETIC] clapping
- いよいよ **iyo-iyo** increasingly
- 手がつけられない **te ga tsukerarenai** out of control, unmanageable
- リボン **ribon** ribbon
- 胸 **mune** chest
- 司会者 **shikaisha** MC (the master of ceremonies)
- アンコール **ankōru** encore
- きっとなる **kitto naru** to look stern
- 答える＝応える **kotaeru** to reply
- 大物 **ōmono** a big piece
- 気が済む **ki ga sumu** to be satisfied
- 挨拶 **aisatsu** greeting
- 呆気にとられる **akke ni torareru** to be taken aback
- 持たせる **motaseru** to make/let someone hold something
- 押し出す **oshidasu** to push out
- 一そう **issō** even more
- …をばかにする **... o baka ni suru** to make fun of ...
- 落ちつく **ochitsuku** to calm down
- 象 **zō** elephant
- 聴衆 **chōshū** audience
- しいんと **shīnto** [MIMETIC] quiet
- 切ない **setsunai** painful, anguish, heartrending
- すばやく **subayaku** fast, quick
- 仲間 **nakama** group members
- 火事 **kaji** fire
- ひっそり **hissori** [MIMETIC] quietly

- やぶれかぶれ **yabure-kabure** desperation, self-abandonment
- 長椅子 **naga-isu** sofa
- どっかり **dokkari** [MIMETIC] flumping (into a chair)
- 足を組む **ashi o kumu** to cross one's legs
- 別に **betsu ni** (nothing) in particular
- 仕上げる **shiageru** to master, to prepare
- 赤ん坊 **akanbō** baby
- 兵隊 **heitai** soldier
- いつでも **itsu de mo** at any time
- 丈夫 **jōbu** strong, healthy
- 普通 **futsū** normal, regular
- 遅く **osoku** late
- 遠く **tōku** far
- がぶがぶ **gabu-gabu** [MIMETIC] gulping down

Exercises

Choose the appropriate item in the parentheses.

1. 六日目の晩に金星音楽団は第六交響曲を首尾よくおわり、拍手が（嵐・風）のように鳴りました。

2. みんな控室に引き上げてきて、楽長はポケットに手を入れて拍手なんか（どう・どこ）でもいいというような顔をしてみんなの間を歩きまわっていました。

3. 司会者が来て、楽長にアンコールの曲か（挨拶・おじぎ）をおねがいしました。

4. でも、楽長はゴーシュに一人で何か弾いてやってくれと言い、みんなはゴーシュにセロを（持って・持たせて）、ゴーシュをステージに押し出しました。

5. ゴーシュがその孔の（あけた・あいた）セロをもって舞台に出ると、みんなはそら見ろというようにもっとひどく手をたたきました。

6. ゴーシュはみんなにひどくばかに（した・された）と思ったので、あの猫の来たときのように怒った象の勢で『印度の虎狩り』を弾きました。

7. ところがみんなは（しいん・きいん）となっていっしょうけんめい聞いていました。

8. ゴーシュは演奏しおわると、すばやくあの（たぬき・猫）のように楽屋ににげ込みました。

9. 楽屋で楽長と仲間はゴーシュに「よかった」（に・と）いったので、ゴーシュはびっくりしました。

10. ゴーシュはその晩おそくうちに帰って、また水をがぶがぶのんで、空をながめ（ながら・と）「ああ、かっこう。あのときはすまなかったなあ。おれは怒ったんじゃなかったんだ。」といいました。

Discussion Questions

1. Why did Gauche decide to play “Tiger Hunting in India”? What was he thinking while he was playing this piece?

2. How do you think each animal helped Gauche to improve his cello skills?

3. Why do you think Gauche thought of the cuckoo?

4. Did your image of the conductor change after reading this section?

5. What kind of messages do you think this story gives us? List as many as you can.

Answer Keys

["Urashima Taro"]

1. 年老いていました 2. は 3. 亀 4. 飲んだり 5. 帰り
6. あけないで 7. ぜんぜん 8. あける 9. 髪 10. 過ごしている

["Snow Woman"]

1. 切り 2. に 3. あって 4. 息 5. 動こう 6. やりました
7. で 8. 生まれました 9. 話して 10. しまいました

["The Spider's Thread"]

Part One : 1. 蓮池 2. ように 3. 地獄 4. つけたり 5. いい 6. やり
7. あげる 8. 銀色 9. なさいました

Part Two : 1. 沈んだり 2. どちら 3. 針 4. 墓 5. さえ 6. 血 7. ばかり
8. 糸 9. 見る 10. 行けば 11. つかみ

Part Three : 1. 地獄 2. 甲斐 3. と 4. 蟻 5. あいた 6. 細い 7. きれ
8. と 9. ぷつりと 10. しまい

Part Four : 1. 始終 2. 沈んで 3. 悲し 4. 地獄 5. 蓮 6. で

["The Siblings Who Almost Drowned"]

Part One : 1. のに 2. に 3. いる 4. こと 5. 聞かないで 6. ので
7. もう 8. ほど

Part Two : 1. 大きい 2. の 3. ざぶり 4. で 5. せっかく 6. に
7. ひどい 8. あそび 9. 立った

Part Three : 1. 高い 2. つく 3. から 4. 行く 5. で 6. つこう 7. して
8. 沖 9. 顔 10. ならない

Part Four : 1. 黙った 2. 沖 3. 岸 4. 見える 5. 沈み 6. 飲んで
7. と 8. 助けて 9. 疲れる

Part Five : 1. する 2. と 3. みる 4. 悲しく 5. 見えませんでした
6. 助けて 7. ぶるぶる 8. ざぶり

Part Six : 1. 小さく 2. 近く 3. きらきら 4. に 5. なったり 6. 岸
7. 這う 8. に 9. 有頂天

Part Seven : 1. へたへた 2. 見る 3. 私 4. 恨んで 5. 立ち 6. 向かって
7. まま 8. よう 9. ので

Part Eight : 1. あり 2. おばあさん 3. うなずいて 4. 心配 5. つもり
6. もって 7. どこ 8. 殺され 9. 動悸が

[“Gauche the Cellist”]

Part One : 1. いう 2. して 3. ながら 4. ぴたり 5. おくれた 6. 糸 7. 教えて

Part Two : 1. そう 2. あわてて 3. ぱたっと 4. どきっと 5. どんと 6. ない 7. と 8. しました 9. 壁

Part Three : 1. ごくごく 2. 虎 3. しまって 4. 重そうに 5. あげる 6. おこり 7. ねられない

Part Four : 1. した 2. 弾き 3. パチパチ 4. 青く 5. タクト 6. 生意気な 7. 舌 8. よう 9. し 10. やり

Part Five : 1. いる 2. から 3. 教わり 4. ちがいます 5. なきました 6. 痛く, いい

Part Six : 1. よう 2. 鳥 3. いきなり 4. どしんと 5. 床 6. ぶつけ 7. あけよう 8. くちばし 9. 落ちた 10. けって

Part Seven : 1. 来て 2. 狸汁 3. 座った 4. スープ 5. もらう 6. とって 7. に 8. と 9. まで

Part Eight : 1. もった 2. 青い 3. 小さくて 4. なおして 5. むっと 6. なれば 7. 床下 8. から 9. 顔

Part Nine : 1. よう 2. 蚊 3. 入れた 4. きれなく 5. やり 6. ぶるぶる 7. 走り 8. 一つまみ

Part Ten : 1. 嵐 2. どう 3. 挨拶 4. 持たせて 5. あいた 6. された 7. しいん 8. 猫 9. と 10. ながら

Authors/Editors/Translators

Anne McNulty is a senior at Stony Brook University. She is enrolled in the Honors College, majors in Linguistics and minors in Asian and Asian American Studies. Anne started attending Japanese classes in the Pre-College Japanese Program at Stony Brook University when she was a high school student. Her research interests include translation studies and Japanese and Korean linguistics. Anne loves reading and translating Japanese and Korean stories.

Eriko Sato is Assistant Professor of Japanese and Translation Studies in the Department of Asian and Asian American Studies at Stony Brook University. She serves as the Director of Asian Languages and the Director of the Teacher Education Program for Japanese. She has authored many Japanese textbooks and supplementary materials including *Contemporary Japanese* (2005/2017, Tuttle).

Illustrator

Rose Goldberg is a senior at Stony Brook University. She majors in Studio Art and Asian and Asian American Studies, and minors in Art History and Japanese Studies. She is also enrolled in the Teacher Education Program for Japanese. Art has been Rose's passion since her childhood, particularly Japanese-style illustrations. She has taken many art courses at the university and enjoys working with different types of mediums.

Acknowledgements

We are grateful to Nancy Goh, Taeko Takeyama and Angie Ang at Tuttle Publishing for their professional assistance and kindness.

—Anne McNulty and Eriko Sato

Published by Tuttle Publishing, an imprint of Periplus Editions (HK) Ltd.

www.tuttlepublishing.com

Illustrations by Rose Goldberg
Audio recordings by Keita Takayama

Library of Congress Control Number: 2018938634

ISBN 978-4-8053-1468-5

First edition
23 22 21 20 10 9 8 7 6 2009VP
Printed in Malaysia

Distributed by

North America, Latin America & Europe
Tuttle Publishing
364 Innovation Drive
North Clarendon, VT 05759-9436 U.S.A.
Tel: 1 (802) 773-8930
Fax: 1 (802) 773-6993
info@tuttlepublishing.com
www.tuttlepublishing.com

Japan
Tuttle Publishing
Yaekari Building, 3rd Floor
5-4-12 Osaki
Shinagawa-ku
Tokyo 141 0032
Tel: (81) 3 5437-0171
Fax: (81) 3 5437-0755
sales@tuttle.co.jp
www.tuttle.co.jp

Asia Pacific
Berkeley Books Pte. Ltd.
3 Kallang Sector #04-01
Singapore 349278
Tel: (65) 6741-2178
Fax: (65) 6741-2179
inquiries@periplus.com.sg
www.tuttlepublishing.com